# WONDROUS WHISPERS OF WISDOM FROM ANCIENT INDIA

*For better life-management in the new millennium*

VOLUME TWO

**Books by V.K. SUBRAMANIAN**

The Upanishads and the Bible

Introspection for India

Sacred Songs of India (Volumes 1, 2, 3, 4, 5, 6)

Wondrous Whispers of Wisdom from Ancient India (Volumes 1 & 2)

The Holistic Way to Health, Happiness and Harmony

Predictive Planets and Presaging Palms

Maxims of Chanakya

Saundaryalahari

The Indian Financial System

Planets, Palms and Predictions

Sivanandalahari

Sri Rudraprasna

Lali and Other Short Stories

Lovetwigs

A Bond to Sorrow

Portraits of Greatness

# WONDROUS WHISPERS OF WISDOM FROM ANCIENT INDIA

*For better life-management in the new millennium*

VOLUME TWO

**V.K. SUBRAMANIAN**

ABHINAV PUBLICATIONS

abhinav publications
New Delhi

First published in India 2002



*Publishers*
Shakti Malik
Abhinav Publications
E-37, Hauz Khas
New Delhi-110016 (INDIA)
Phones: 6566387, 6562784, 6524658
Fax: 91-11-6857009
e-mail: shakti@nde.vsnl.net.in
Website: http//www.abhinavexports.com

ISBN 81-7017-395-7 (Set)
ISBN 81-7017-409-0 (Vol. II)

*Lasertypeset by*
S.R. Enterprises
New Delhi-110024

*Printed at* D.K. Fine Art Press Pvt. Ltd.
Ashok Vihar, Delhi

*To*
*Girija, my beloved wife, who has stood*
*by my side through thick and thin*
*for forty-seven years of a wonderful*
*married life*

"If I were asked under what sky the human mind has most fully developed some of its choicest gifts, has most deeply pondered on the great problems of life, and has found solutions of some of them which will deserve the attention even of those who have studied Plato and Kant—I should point to India.

And if I were to ask myself from what literature we here in Europe, we who have been nurtured almost exclusively on the thoughts of Greeks and Romans, and of one Semitic race, the Jewish may draw that corrective which is most wanted in order to make our inner life more perfect, more comprehensive, more universal, in fact more truly human, a life, not for this life only, but a transfigured and eternal life—again I should point to India."

*—Max Muller*

# CONTENTS

# ACKNOWLEDGEMENTS

I am indebted to the Kerala Sahitya Academy, whose publication *Subhāshitasahasri* helped me in the selections from *Panchatantra* and *Hitopadesa.*

I am grateful to my friend, Mrs. B. Jayalakshmi, who selected the verses from Tirukkural.

I would also like to thank Swami Jagadeesvarananda Sarasvati whose commentary on *Sukranitisāra* was useful in the writing of this book.

My thanks are also due to my wife Mrs. Girija Subramanian who wrote out the passages from *Tirukkural* in Tamil so as to enable me to write them in the Devanagari script.

I am also grateful, as usual, to my publisher Shakti Malik who brings out my books so well.

**V.K. SUBRAMANIAN**

# KEY TO TRANSLITERATION AND PRONUNCIATION

| Devanagari letter | Transliterated as | Sounds like |
|---|---|---|
| अ | a | o in son |
| आ | ā or aa | a in master |
| इ | i | i in if |
| ई | ī or ee | ee in feel |
| उ | u | u in full |
| ऊ | ū or oo | oo in boot |
| ऋ | ṛ or ri | somewhat between r & ri |
| ए | e | ay in May |
| ऐ | ai | y in my |
| ओ | o | o in oh |
| औ | au | ow in now |
| अः | ḥ | h in oh |
| क | k | k in keen |
| ख | kh | ckh in blackhead |
| ग | g | g in go |
| घ | gh | gh in loghout |
| ङ | ṅ | ṅ in singer |
| च | ch | ch in chart |
| छ | cch | ch in chain |
| ज | j | j in judge |
| झ | jh | dgeh in hedgehog |
| ञ | ñ | n (somewhat) in French |

| Devanagari letter | Transliterated as | Sounds like |
|---|---|---|
| ट | ṭ | t in ten |
| ठ | ṭh | th in anthill |
| ड | ḍ | d in den |
| ढ | ḍh | dh in childhood |
| ण | ṇ | n in under |
| त | t | t in French |
| थ | th | th in thumb |
| द | d | th in mother |
| धा | dh | th in breathe |
| न | n | n in not |
| प | p | p in pen |
| फ | ph | ph in loophole |
| ब | b | b in bag |
| भ | bh | bh in abhor |
| म | m | m in mother |
| य | y | y in yard |
| र | r | r in run |
| ल | l | l in luck |
| व | v | v in avert |
| श | ś | sh in reich |
| ष | ṣ or sh | sh in show |
| स | s | s in sun |
| ह | h | h in hot |
| ळ | ḷ | ll in pull |
| ऴ | zh | j in jean (French) |

# INTRODUCTION

WONDROUS WHISPERS OF WISDOM FROM ANCIENT INDIA VOLUME TWO continues the picking of pearls from the vast unsavoured treasures of the literary heritage of ancient India which commenced in Volume One.

The selections in the first volume included words of wisdom orally handed down the centuries known as *Subhāshitās* (wellspoken words) and works of three great Masters of the Sanskrit language: *Veda Vyasa* (author of Mahabharata), *Sankaracharya* (the advaitic philosopher), and *Bhartṛhari* (the philosopher-king of Ujjain).

The selections in this volume include maxims from four great works of antiquity: *Panchatantra, Hitopadesa, Tirukkural* and *Sukraniti.*

The *Panchatantra* is a collection of stories and legends, in five books compiled by an author known as Vishnusarman. Dr. Hertel, the famous indological scholar, believes that the original work was composed in Kashmir, about 200 B.C., though many of the stories in it were already wellknown.

*Panchatantra* was first translated from Sanskrit in the 6th century A.D. by Buzerchumihr. There have been several translations and revised editions since then, one of the most wellknown being that by Arthur W. Ryder, the wellknown American Oriental scholar.

The *Panchatantra* stories, like the *Aesop's fables,* have tried to preach codes of conduct that make life richer and happier and more meaningful.

In the words of Ryder, "The noble ideal of the harmonious development of the powers of man, a life in which security, prosperity, resolute action, friendship, and good learning are so combined as to produce joy, is presented in an artistic form of perfect fitness, in five books of wise and witty stories, in most of which the actors are animals."

The *Hitopadesa* (lit. Sound Advice), whose authorship is attributed to Narayana, is mainly derived from the Panchatantra—though it draws upon other works as well—and aims at teaching the principles of polity, guided by ethics. According to Prof. H. Morley, "The *Hitopadesa* comes to us, from a far place and time, as a manual of worldly wisdom."

The *Tirukkural,* the third work from which selections have been included in this volume, is an ancient Tamil classic, created by Tiruvalluvar, who lived in the second century B.C. according to Oriental scholars and 5th century A.D. according to Western critics.

Tiruvalluvar was a weaver by profession and lived a contented householder's life with his devoted wife Vasuki.

Biographical details about Tiruvalluvar's life are scanty but his work has been with us for nearly 2000 years, preaching moral values of a high ethical order.

The *Tirukkural* contains 1330 maxims, in 133 chapters of ten couplets each.

Albert Schweitzer, the great philosopher, said of this Tamil *magnum opus*: "With sure strokes, the *Kural* draws the ideal of simple ethical humanity. On the most varied questions concerning the conduct of man to himself and to the world its utterances are characterised by nobility and good sense. There hardly exists in the literature of the world a collection of maxims in which we find such lofty wisdom."

Mahatma Gandhi considered the *Tirukkural* as one of the highest and purest expressions of human thought.

*Sukraniti* or *Sukranitisāra* is an ancient work attributed to Sukracharya, an ancient sage well versed in the art of polity, but the work has undergone several recensions and the work in its present form is assigned to the 8th century A.D. by scholars like Dr. Altekar.

Though like the other three works, *Sukraniti* also offers advice on the general conduct of life, the emphasis is more on counsel for rulers and how they should conduct the affairs of state, which would be equally valid and valuable for modern chief executives and tycoons of business.

In short, we have in this volume a rich and varied fare, which will give practical guidance and lift up the spirits of all: business executives and professionals, educationists, social reformers and public men and women who are stressed out by the intractable problems and frightening dilemmas facing the society.

**V.K. SUBRAMANIAN**

# PART ONE

# WONDROUS WHISPERS OF WISDOM FROM PANCHATANTRA

## WONDROUS WHISPERS OF WISDOM FROM PANCHATANTRA

## AFFECTION

ददाति प्रतिगृह्णाति गुह्यमाख्याति पृच्छति
भुङ्क्ते भोजयते चैवं षड्विधं प्रीतिलक्षणं।।

Dadaati pratigrhnaati guhyamaakhyaati prcchati
Bhungte bhojayate chaivam shadvidham preetilakshanam.

## ALCOHOL

वैकल्यं धरणीपातम्
यथोचितजल्पनं
सन्निपातस्य चिह्नानि
मद्यं सर्वत्र दर्शयेत्।।

Vaikalyam dharaneepaatam
Yathochitajalpanam
Sannipaatasya chihnāni
Madyam sarvatra darśayet.

## BAD THINGS

कलहान्तानि हर्म्याणि कुवाक्यान्तं च सौहृदं
कुराजान्तानि राष्ट्राणि कुकर्मान्तं यशो नृणां।।

Kalahaantaani harmyaaṇi kuvaakyaantam cha sauhṛdam
Kuraajaantaani raashṭraaṇi kukarmāntam yaśo nṛṇām.

## BIRTH

परिवर्तिनि संसारे मृतः को वा न जायते
जातस्तु गण्यते सोऽत्र यः स्फुरत्यन्वयाधिकं।।

Parivartini samsaare mṛtaḥ ko vaa na jaayate
Jaatastu gaṇyate soatra yaḥ sphuratyanvayaadhikam.

## AFFECTION

Six are the signs of affection:
Gives, receives, tells secrets, questions, eats, feeds.

## ALCOHOL

Ugliness in appearance, falling down on the floor, speaking incoherently, these signs of downfall, alcohol will display everywhere.

## BAD THINGS

Quarrels bring down mansions,
Bad words break up friendships,
Bad rulers destroy nations,
Bad deeds destroy men's reputations.

## BIRTH

In this revolving phenomenal world, who that dies is not born again?
He is deemed as really born, who outshines others.

## BRAVERY

दर्शितभयेऽपि धातरि धैर्यध्वंसो भवेन्न धीराणां
शोषितसरसि निदाघे नितरामेवोद्धतः सिन्धुः।।

Darśitabhayeapi dhaatari dhairyadhvamso bhavenna dheeraaṇaam
Śoshitasarasi nidaaghe nitaraamevoddhataḥ sindhuḥ.

## CAPTIVATION

उत्तमं प्रणिपातेन शूरं भेदेन योजयेत्
नीचमिष्टप्रदानेन इष्टं धर्मेण योजयेत्।।

Uttamam praṇipaatena śooram bhedena yojayet
Neechamishṭapradaanena ishṭam dharmeṇa yojayet.

## DEATH

जीवन्तोऽपि मृता पञ्च व्यासेन परिकीर्तिताः
दरिद्रो व्याधितो मूर्खः प्रवासी नित्यसेवकः।।

Jeevantoapi mṛtaa pañcha vyaasena parikeertitaaḥ
Daridro vyaadhito moorkhaḥ pravaasee nityasevakaḥ

## DONATION

उपार्जितानां वित्तानां त्याग एव हि रक्षणं
तडागोदरसंस्थानां परीवाह इवांभसा।।

Upaarjitaanaam vittaanaam tyaaga eva hi rakshaṇam
Taḍaagodarasamsthaanaam pareevaaha ivaambhasaa.

## BRAVERY

Even when the creator strikes fear, the brave do not lose their courage,
Even in summer which dries up the ponds, the ocean remains swollen.

## CAPTIVATION

The superior one should be made friendly by prostration,
The hero should be tamed by division,
The low one by giving whatever he wants,
And the friend by righteous deed.

## DEATH

It has been proclaimed by Vyāsa that five are deemed dead, even if alive:
The povertystricken, the diseased, the idiot, the one who lives abroad and the one who has to be a permanent servant.

## DONATION

Donation is the best protection of money earned,
just like the outlet for the waters of a pond.

## EFFORT

उद्यमेन हि सिद्धयन्ति कार्याणि न मनोरथैः
न हि सुप्तस्य सिंहस्य प्रविशन्ति मुखे मृगाः।।

Udyamena hi siddhyanti kaaryaaṇi na manorathaiḥ
Na hi suptasya simhasya praviśanti mukhe mṛgaaḥ.

## ENMITY

बलोपपन्नोऽपि हि बुद्धिमान् नरः
परं नयेन्न स्वयमेव वैरितां
भिषक् ममास्तीति विचिन्त्य भक्षये-
दकारणात् को हि विचक्षणो विषं।।

Balopapanno'pi hi buddhimaan naraḥ
Param nayenna svayameva vairitaam
Bhishak mamāsteeti vichintya bhakshaye-
dakaaraṇaat ko hi vichakshaṇo visham.

बहुर्भिन विरोद्धव्यं दुर्जनैः स्वजनैरपि
स्फुरन्तमपि नागेन्द्रं भक्षयन्ति पिपीलिकाः।।

Bahurbhina viroddhavyam durjanaiḥ svajanairapi
Sphurantamapi naagendram bhakshayanti pipeelikaaḥ.

## FIGHT

अविदित्वा मनःशक्तिं परस्य च समत्सुकः
गच्छन्नभिमुखे वह्नौ नाशं याति पतंगवत्।।

Aviditvaa manaḥśaktim parasya cha samutsukaḥ
Gacchannabhimukhe vahnau naaśam yaati patangavat.

## EFFORT

Tasks can be achieved only by effort,
not by mere dreaming,
Animals do not enter the mouth of a sleeping lion.

## ENMITY

The wise one, even if he is strong, should not lead (by his actions) his enemy to greater enmity.
Which wise one will drink poison, feeling secure that "I have a captive physician".

One should not have enmity with many enemies, whether they are good or bad,
Ants can eat up even an elephant.

## FIGHT

Without knowing the mental prowess of the enemy, he who goes to fight, out of zeal, gets destroyed like the moth flying

महद्भि: स्पर्धमानस्य विपदेव गरीयसी
दन्तभंगो हि नागानां श्लाघ्यो गिरिविदारणे।।

Mahadbhiḥ spardhamaanasya vipadeva gareeyasee
Dantabhango hi naagaanaam ślaaghyo girividaaraṇe.

## FOOLS

उपदेशो हि मूर्खानां प्रकोपाय न शान्तये
पय:पानं भुजंगस्य केवलं विषवर्धनं।।

Upadeśo hi moorkhaanam prakopaaya na śaantaye
Payappaanam bhujangasya kevalam vishavardhanam.

## FRIENDSHIP

इक्षोरग्रात् क्रमश:
पर्वणि पर्वणि यथा रसविशेष:
तद्वत् सज्जनमैत्री
विपरीतानां तु विपरीता।।

Ikshoragraat kramaśaḥ
Parvaṇi parvaṇi yathaa rasaviśeshaḥ
Tadvat sajjanamaitree
Vipareetaanaam tu vipareetaa.

ययोरेव समं वित्तं ययोरेव समं कुलं
तयोर्मैत्री विवाहश्च न तु पुष्ट विपुष्टयो:।।

Yayoreva samam vittam yayoreva samam kulam
Tayormaitree vivāhaścha na tu pushṭa vipushṭayoḥ.

into the fire.
In fighting against great ones, even if one meets with calamities, that is an honour.
When elephants try to tear apart mountains, if their tusks get broken, even that is praiseworthy.

## FOOLS

Advice only infuriates fools, it does not pacify them.
Drinking milk only increases the poison in the snake.

## FRIENDSHIP

The sugarcane becomes sweeter and sweeter, as you go down gradually from the top crossing each knot,
So too is the friendship with good ones.
The opposite is the case with evil ones.

Only among those who are equal in wealth and family status, should there be friendship and marital alliance; not between those who are disparate in these.

## FRUITFULNESS

जातस्य नदीतीरे तस्यापि तृणस्य जन्मसाफल्यम्
यत्सलिलमग्नाकुलजनहस्तालम्बनं भवति।।

Jaatasya nadee teere tasyaapi tṛṇasya janmasaaphalyam
Yatsalilamagnākulajanahastaalambanam bhavati.

## GREED

इच्छति शती सहस्त्रं
ससहस्त्रः कोटिमीहते कर्तुं
कोटियुतोऽपि नृपत्वं
नृपोऽपि बत चक्रवर्तित्वं।।

Icchati śatee sahasram
Sasahasraḥ koṭimeehate kartum
Koṭiyutoapi nṛpatvam
Nṛpoapi bata chakravartitvam.

## HARSH WORDS

रोहते सायकैर्विद्धं वनं परशुना हतं
वाचा दुरुक्तं बीभत्सं न संरोहति वाक्क्षतं।।

Rohate saayakaīrviddham vanam paraśunaa hatam
Vaachaa duruktam beebhatsam na samrohati vākkshatam.

## HELP

उपकारिषु यः साधुः साधुत्वे तस्य को गुणः
अपकारिषु यः साधुः स साधुसद्भिरुच्यते।।

Upakaarishu yaḥ saadhuḥ saadhutve tasya ko guṇaḥ
Apakaarishu yaḥ saadhuḥ sa saadhusadbhiruchyate.

## FRUITFULNESS

Even the grass which grows on the river bank has a fruitful life,
Since it offers support to the hands of persons in danger of being drowned in water.

## GREED

The one who has a hundred thirsts for a thousand,
The one who has a thousand thirsts for the millions,
The one who has million thirsts for ruling power,
The ruler thirsts to be an emperor.

## HARSH WORDS

That which is wounded with arrows, and cut down by the axe grows,
But the wound inflicted on the heart by harsh words does not heal.

## HELP

What quality is there in one who helps persons who reciprocate the help.
He who helps one who does harm is really an admirably good person.

## IDEAL ONES

स सुहृद् व्यसने यः स्यात् स पुत्रो यस्तु भक्तिमान्
स भृत्यो यो विधेयज्ञः सा भार्या यत्र निर्वृतिः।।

Sa suhṛd vyasane yaḥ syaat sa putro yastu bhaktimaan
Sa bhṛtyo yo vidheyajñaḥ saa bhaaryaa yatra nirvṛtiḥ.

## INEVITABILITY

कोऽर्थान् प्राप्य न गर्वितो भुवि नरः कस्यापदोस्तं गताः
स्त्रीभिः कस्य न खण्डितं बत मनः को नाम राज्ञां प्रियः
कः कालस्य न गोचरो धनकृते कोऽर्थी गतो गौरवं
को वा दुर्जनवागुरानिपतितः क्षेमेण यातो गृहं।।

Koarthaan praapya na garvito bhuvi naraḥ kasyāpadostam gataaḥ?
Streebhiḥ kasya na khaṇḍitam bata manaḥ ko naama raajñām priyaḥ?
Kaḥ kaalasya na gocharo dhanakṛte koarthee gato gauravam?
Ko vaa durjanavaaguraanipatitaḥ kshemeṇa yāto gṛham?

## INGRATITUDE

ब्रह्मघ्ने च सुरापे च चोरे भग्नव्रते तथा
निष्कृतिर्विहिता लोके कृतघ्ने नास्ति निष्कृतिः।।

Brahmaghne cha suraape cha chore bhagnavrate tathaa
Nishkṛtirvihitaa loke kṛtaghne naasti nishkritiḥ.

## INTERFERENCE

अव्यापारेषु व्यापारं यो नरः कर्तुमिच्छति
स एव निधनं याति कीलोत्पाटीव वानरः।।

Avyaapaareshu vyaapāram yo naraḥ kartumicchati
Sa eva nidhanam yaati keelotpaaṭeeva vānaraḥ.

## IDEAL ONES

He is the friend who helps in difficulties,
He is the son who is devoted,
He is the servant who carries out orders,
She is the wife, who is satisfied.

## INEVITABILITY

In this world, who, on attaining wealth, has not become arrogant?
Whom have difficulties stopped to bother?
Whose hearts have not been broken by women?
Who has been the permanent favourite of rulers?
Who has not succumbed to time?
Who has maintained dignity, after begging for money?
Who, caught in the net of wicked ones, has reached home safe?

## INGRATITUDE

Expiation has been prescribed for the following sinners:
He who killed a Brahmin, the alcoholic, the thief and the one who breaks vows.
But there is no expiation for the ungrateful one.

## INTERFERENCE

A man who wishes to meddle with matters which do not concern him, meets with destruction like the monkey which pulled the wedge.

## KARMA

यथा धेनुसहस्त्रेषु वत्सो विन्दति मातरं
तथा पूर्वकृतं कर्म कर्तारमनुगच्छति।।

Yathaa dhenusahasreshu vatso vindati maataram
Tathaa poorvakṛtam karma kartaaramanugacchati.

## LIVELIHOOD

कृता भिक्षोरकैर्वितरति नृपो नोचितरहो
कृषिः क्लिष्टा विद्या गुरुविनयवृत्त्यातिविषमा
कुमीदाद्दारिद्रयं परकरगतग्रन्थिशमना-
न्न मन्ये वाणिज्यात्किमपि परमं वर्तनमिह।।

Kṛtaa bhikshorakairvitarati nṛpo nochitaraho
Kṛshiḥ klishṭaa vidyaa guruvinayavrittyaativishamaa.
Kumeedaaddaaridrayam parakaragatagranthiśamanaa-
nna manye vaaṇijyaatkimapi paramam vartanamiha.

## LIVING

यस्मिन् जीवति जीवन्ति बहवः सोऽत्र जीवति
वयांसि किं न कुर्वन्ति चञ्चा स्वोदरपूरणं।।

Yasmin jeevati jeevanti bahavaḥ soatra jeevati
Vayaamsi kim na kurvanti chañchaa svodarapooraṇam.

## LOSS

सर्वनाशे समुत्पन्नेह्यदर्धं त्यजति पण्डितः
अर्धेन कुरुते कार्यं सर्वनाशो न जायते।।

Sarvanaaśe samutpannehyadardham tyajati paṇḍitaḥ
Ardhena kurute kaaryam sarvanaaśo na jaayate.

## KARMA

Just as a calf locates its mother among a thousand cows,
Accumulated Karma of the past pursues the doer.

## LIVELIHOOD

Begging is resorted to by the lowly,
The ruler does not pay adequate compensation,
Farming involves a lot of labour,
Learning is difficult, since it involves serving the teacher with humility,
Moneylending leads to poverty, due to loss of money given to others,
I think there is no better method of earning one's livelihood than trading.

## LIVING

He lives, by whose living many live,
Birds with their beaks fill their own stomachs.

## LOSS

When loss of everything is imminent, the wise one gives up half,
With half, he accomplishes the task. Everything is not lost.

## MONEY

अर्थार्थी जीवलोकोऽयं श्मशानमपि सेवते
जनितारमपि त्यक्त्वा निस्वं गच्छति दूरः।।

Arthaarthee jeevaloko'yam śmaśaanamapi sevate
Janitaaramapi tyaktvaa nisvam gacchati doorah̤.

यस्यार्थास्तस्य मित्राणि
यस्यार्थास्तस्य बान्धवाः
यस्यार्था स पुमान् लोके
यस्यार्थः स च पण्डितः।।

Yasyaarthaastasya mitraaṇi
Yasyaarthaastasya baandhavaaḥ
Yasyaarthaa sa pumaan loke
Yasyaarthaḥ sa cha paṇḍitaḥ.

अर्थेन तु विहीनस्य पुरुषस्याल्पमेधसः
क्रिया सर्वा विनश्यन्ति ग्रीष्मे कुसरितो यथा।।

Arthena tu viheenasya purushasyaalpamedhasaḥ
Kriyaa sarvaa vinaśyanti greeshme kusarito yathaa.

पूज्यते यदपूज्योपि यदगम्योपि गम्यते
वन्द्यते यदवन्द्योपि सप्रभावो धनस्य च।।

Poojyate yadapoojyopi yadagamyopi gamyate
Vandyate yadavandyopi sa prabhaavo dhanasya cha.

अशनादेन्द्रियाणीव स्युः कार्यान्यखिलान्यपि
एतस्यात्कारणाद्वित्तं सर्वसाधनमुच्यते।।

Aśanaadendriyaaṇeeva syuḥ kaaryaanyakhilanyapi
Etasyaatkaaraṇaadvittam sarvasaadhanamuchyate.

## MONEY

One seeking money will reside even in the funeral ground. He will go even to a far-off place, giving up his own destitute father.

He who has money has friends,
He who has money has relations,
He who has money is a person to reckon with,
He who has money is a learned one!

The efforts of a person devoid of money or intellect
come to naught like the (waterless) rivers in summer.

The one unworthy of respect is respected,
The one who is unworthy of being approached is approached,
The one who is unworthy of salutation is saluted,
Such is the power of money!

All senses are invigorated by eating, so too all actions by wealth.
Hence is it said: Money is the means to achieve everything.

## MOTHER

निरतिशयं गरिमाणं तेन जनन्याः स्मरन्ति विद्वांसः
यत्कमपि वहति गर्भे महतामपि यो गुरुर्भवति।।

Niratiśayam garimaaṇam tena jananyaaḥ smaranti vidwaamsaḥ
Yatkamapi vahati garbhe mahataamapi yo gururbhavati.

## PERFUMES

पण्यानां गान्धिकं पण्यं किमन्यैः काञ्चनादिभिः
यत्रैकेन च यत्क्रीतं तच्छतेन प्रदीयते।।

Paṇyaanaam gaandhikam paṇyam kimanyaiḥ kaañchanaadibhiḥ
Yatraikena cha yatkreetam tacchatena pradeeyate.

## POSITION

नक्रः स्वस्थानमासाद्य गजेन्द्रमपि कर्षति
स एव प्रच्युतो स्थानाच्छुनापि परिभूयते।।

Nakraḥ svasthaanamaasaadya gajendramapi karshati
Sa eva prachyuto sthaanaacchunaapi paribhooyate.

## PROTECTION

सर्वनाशे च संजाते प्राणानामपि संशये
अपि शत्रुं प्रणम्योच्चैः रक्षेत् प्राणान् धनानि च।।

Sarvanaaśe cha samjaate praaṇaanaamapi samśaye
Api śatrum praṇamyocchaiḥ rakshet praaṇaan dhanaani cha.

## MOTHER

Learned ones admit the unequalled greatness of a mother, since she bears a foetus in the womb, which, when born, is venerated even by the great.

## PERFUMES

Of all merchandise for sale, perfumes are the best!
Not commodities like gold.
Perfumes bought for one can be sold for hundred!

## POSITION

The crocodile, when it is in its own place, is capable of grabbing even the wild elephant!
When it is out of place, it is dragged even by the dog!

## PROTECTION

When the loss of everything is imminent and life itself is in danger, even by bowing to the enemy, life and wealth should be protected.

## RESIDENCE

यस्मिन् देशे न सम्मानो न प्रीतिर्न च बान्धवाः
न च विद्यागमः कश्चिन्न तत्र दिवसं न येत्।।

Yasmin deśe na sammaano na preetirna cha baandhavaaḥ
Na cha vidyaagamaḥ kaśchinna tatra divasam na yet.

## RULER

यस्मिन्नेवाधिकं चक्षुरारोपयति पार्थिवः
अकुलीनः कुलीनो वा स श्रियो भाजनं नरः।।

Yasminnevaadhikam chakshuraaropayati paarthivaḥ
Akuleenaḥ kuleeno vaa sa śriyo bhaajanam naraḥ.

## SELF-INTEREST

वृक्षं क्षीणफलं त्यजन्ति विहगाः शुष्कं सरः सारसाः
निर्द्रव्यं पुरुषं त्यजन्ति गणिकाः भ्रष्टं नृपं मन्त्रिणः
पुष्पं परयुषितं त्यजन्ति मधुपाः दग्धं वनान्तं मृगाः
सर्वं कार्यवशाज्जनोऽभिरमते तत् कस्य को वल्लभः।।

Vriksham ksheeṇaphalam tyajanti vihagaaḥ sushkam saraḥ saarasaaḥ
Nirdravyam purusham tyajanti gaṇikaaḥ bhrashṭam nṛpam mantriṇaḥ
Pushpam parayushitam tyajanti madhupaaḥ dagdham vanaantam mṛgaaḥ
Sarvam kaaryavaśaajjanoabhiramate tat kasya ko vallabhaḥ.

## RESIDENCE

Where there is no respect, no means of happiness,
no relations and no scope for acquiring learning, one should not stay even for a day.

## RULER

He, in whom the ruler is specially interested, becomes prosperous, be he born in a high family or a low one.

## SELF-INTEREST

The birds desert trees when fruits diminish,
the swans desert dried up ponds,
hookers desert moneyless men,
counsellors desert the ruler who has lost his kingdom,
the bees desert drooping flowers,
animals desert burntout jungles,
People show affection out of self-interest,
Really, who is fond of whom?

## SERVICE

अरण्यरुधितं कृतं शवशरीरमुद्वर्त्तितं
स्थलेब्जमवरोपितं सुचिरमूषरे वर्षितं
श्वपुच्छमवनमितं बधिर कर्ण जापः कृतो
धृतोन्धमुखदर्प्पणो यदबुधो जनः सेवितः।।

Araṇyarudhitam kṛtam śavaśareeramudvarttitam
Sthalebjamavaropitam suchiramooshare varshitam
Śvapucchamavanamitam badhirakarṇajāpaḥ kṛto
Dhṛtoandhamukhadarppaṇo yadabudho janaḥ sevitaḥ.

## SHINE

नागो भाति मदेन कं जलरुहैः पूर्णेन्दुना शर्वरी
शीलेन प्रमदा जवेन तुरगो नित्योत्सवैर्मन्दिरं
वाणी व्याकरणेन हंसमिथुनैर्नद्यः सभा पण्डितैः
सत्पुत्रेण कुलं नृपेण वसुधा लोकत्रयं विष्णुना।।

Naago bhaati madena kam jalaruhaiḥ poorṇendunaa śarvaree
Śeelena pramadaa javena turago nityotsavairmandiram
Vāṇee vyaakaraṇena hamsamithunairnadyaḥ sabhaa paṇḍitaiḥ
Satputreṇa kulam nṛpeṇa vasudhaa lokatrayam vishṇunaa.

## SILENCE

आत्मनो मुखदोषेण बध्यन्ते शुकसारिकाः
बकास्तत्र न बध्यन्ते मौनं सर्वार्थसाधकं।।

Aatmano mukhadosheṇa badhyante śukasaarikaaḥ
Bakaastatra na badhyante maunam sarvaarthasaadhakam.

## SERVICE

Serving someone without sense or good qualities is like:
crying in the wilderness,
applying perfume to a corpse,
planting the lotus on land,
raining on saline soil,
trying to make the dog's tail straight,
speaking into the ears of the deaf,
and showing the mirror to the blind
(absolutely useless)!

## SHINE

the elephant shines by its rut,
water shines by lotuses,
the night by the full moon,
woman shines by her character,
the horse shines by its speed,
the house by daily rituals,
speech shines by correct grammar,
the rivers shine by pairs of swans,
the assembly shines by learned scholars,
the family shines by a good son,
the land shines by the ruler,
the three worlds by the omnipresent God.

## SILENCE

Because of their capacity to speak, birds like parrots are caged.
The cranes (which are silent) are not caged.
Silence achieves all goals.

## SON

सम्पदि यस्य न हर्षो
विपदि विषादो रणे न भीरुत्वं
तं भुवन त्रयतिलकं
जनयति जननी सुतं विरळं।।

Sampadi yasya na harsho
Vipadi vishaado raṇe na bheerutvam
Tam bhuvanatrayatilakam
Janayati jananee sutam viraḷam.

## SORROWSHARING

स्वामिनि गुणान्तरज्ञे
गुणवति भृत्येऽनुसारिणि कळत्रे
मित्रे चानुपचर्ये
निवेद्य दुःखं सुखी भवति।।

Swaamini guṇaantarajñe
Guṇavati bhṛtyeanusaariṇi kaḷatre
Mitre chaanupacharye
Nivedya duḥkham sukhee bhavati.

सुहृदि निरन्तर चित्ते
गुणवति भृत्ये प्रियासु नारीषु
स्वामिनि शक्तिसमेते
निवेद्य दुःखं जनः सुखी भवति।।

Suhṛdi nirantara chitte
Guṇavati bhṛtye priyaasu nāreeshu
Swaamini śaktisamete
Nivedya duḥkham janaḥ sukhee bhavati.

## SON

He who does not rejoice in prosperity
nor feels sad in difficulties and is not afraid of a fight, and
is an adornment for the three worlds,
Such a son, only a very few mothers can give birth to.

## SORROWSHARING

Anyone can be happy, if he is able to share sorrow with:
an understanding master,
a good servant,
an obedient wife,
and an affectionate friend.

One gets solace and satisfaction when one shares one's sorrow with:
a dear friend,
a good servent,
affectionate women,
and a strong master.

## SUPERIOR ONE

गुणवत्तरपात्रेण छाद्यन्ते गुणिनो गुणाः
रात्रौ दीपशिखाकान्तिर्न भानावुदिते सति।।

Guṇavattarapaatreṇa cchaadyante guṇino guṇaaḥ
Raatrau deepaśikhaakaantirna bhānaavudite sati.

## TASK

अपमानं पुरस्कृत्य मानं कृत्वा तु पृष्ठतः
स्वकार्यमुद्धरेत् प्राज्ञः कार्यध्वंसो हि मूर्खता।।

Apamaanam puraskṛtya maanam kṛtvaa tu pṛshṭhataḥ
Svakāryamuddharet praajñaḥ kaaryadhvamso hi moorkhataa.

## TRANSIENCE

अभ्रच्छाया खलप्रीतिर्नवसस्यानि योषितः
किंचित्कालोपभोग्यानि यौवनानि धनानि च।।

Abhracchaayaa khalapreetirnavasasyaani yoshitaḥ
Kimchitkaalopabhogyaani yauvanaani dhanaani cha.

## TROUBLEMAKER

अकृतोपद्रवः कश्चिन्महानपि न पूज्यते
अर्चयन्ति नराः नागं न तार्क्ष्यं न गजादिकं।।

Akṛtopadravaḥ kaśchinmahaanapi na poojyate
Archayanti naraaḥ naagam na taarkshyam na gajādikam.

## SUPERIOR ONE

The qualities of a person are shadowed by persons of superior qualities,
At night the lamp's wick shines, not after the sun rises.

## TASK

Disregarding disrespect and giving backseat to pride, the wise one accomplishes his task. Disrupting a task is idiocy.

## TRANSIENCE

The shade provided by clouds, the pleasure of the wicked, fresh plants, women, youth, wealth—all these can be enjoyed only for a short while.

## TROUBLEMAKER

Even if one is great, if one does not have the power to trouble, he is not venerated!
People worship the snake, not the kite or the elephant.

## TRUST

यस्य न ज्ञायते शीलं कुलं विद्या नरस्य च
कस्तेन सह विश्वासं पुमान् कुर्याद्विचक्षणः।।

Yasya na jñaayate śeelam kulam vidyaa narasya cha
Kastena saha viśvaasam pumaan kuryaadvichakshaṇaḥ.

## UNION

मृगाः मृगैः संगमनुव्रजन्ति
गावश्च गोभिस्तुरंगास्तुरंगैः
मूर्खाश्च मूर्खैः सुधियः सुधीभिः
समानशीलव्यसनेषु सख्यं।।

Mṛgaaḥ mṛgaiḥ samgamanuvrajanti
Gaavaścha gobhisturangāsturangaiḥ
Moorkhaaścha moorkhaiḥ sudhiyaḥ sudheebhiḥ
Samaanaśeelavyasaneshu sakhyam.

## WEALTH

मानो वा दर्पो वा विज्ञानं विभ्रमं सुबुद्धिर्वा
सर्वं प्रणश्यति समं वित्तविहीनो यदा पुरुषः।।

Maano vaa darpo vaa vijñaanam vibhramam subuddhirvaa
Sarvam praṇaśyati samam vittaviheeno yadaa purushaḥ.

अर्थेभ्योऽपि हि वृद्धेभ्यः संदत्तेभ्यस्ततस्ततः
प्रवर्तन्ते क्रियाः सर्वाः पर्वतेभ्य इवापगाः।।

Arthebhyoapi hi vṛddhebhyaḥ samdattebhyastatastataḥ
Pravartante kriyaaḥ sarvaaḥ parvatebhya ivaapagaaḥ.

## TRUST

How can a wise person trust one, whose lineage, learning and character are not known?

## UNION

Deer seek union with deer,
Cows with cows, horses with horses,
Fools with fools, and learned ones with learned ones.
Union takes place between those who are equal in character and interests.

## WEALTH

Respect, pride, wisdom, beauty, good intellect everything disappears the moment a person loses wealth.

All acts are rendered possible by wealth, enhanced and well accumulated, like the rivers flowing down from mountains.

सोपायाना च सर्वेषामुपायः पण्यसंग्रहः
धनार्थं शस्यते ह्येकस्तदन्यः संशयात्मकः।।

Sopaayaanaa cha sarveshaamupaayaḥ paṇyasamgrahaḥ
Dhanaartham śasyate hyekastadanyaḥ samśayaatmakaḥ.

न वित्तं दर्शयेत् प्राज्ञः
कस्यचित् स्वल्पमप्यहो
मुनेरपियतस्तस्य
दर्शनाच्चलितं मनः।।

Na vittam darśayet praajñaḥ
Kasyachit svalpamapyaho
Munerapiyatastasya
Darśanaacchalitam manaḥ.

गृहमध्यनिखातेन धनेन रमते यदि
स तु तेनानुसारेण रमते किं नु मेरुणा।।

Gṛhamadhyanikhaatena dhanena ramate yadi
Sa tu tenaanusaareṇa ramate kim nu meruṇaa.

उत्साहसम्पन्नमदीर्घसूत्रं
क्रियाविधिज्ञं व्यसनेष्वसक्तं
शूरं कृतज्ञं दृढसौहृदं च
लक्ष्मीः स्वयं याति निवासहेतोः।।

Utsaahasampannamadeerghasootram
Kriyaavidhijñam vyasaneshvasaktam
Śooram kṛtajñam dṛḍhasauhṛidam cha
Lakshmeeḥ svayam yaati nivaasahetoḥ.

Storing up merchandise is the best means of accumulating wealth. All other means are of doubtful value.

The wise one should not disclose his wealth, however small it may be,
Since even a sage's mind will be affected by the sight of wealth.

If one can derive happiness from wealth kept underground in the house, one might as well be happy with Mount Meru (which is supposed to be a gold mine)!

The goddess of wealth, on her own, seeks residence in that individual who is:
enthusiastic,
does not procrastinate,
does prescribed tasks at the right time,
is not addicted to sensory pleasures,
is courageous,
grateful,
and strong in his friendship.

## WICKED ONES

कृते प्रतिकृतिं कुर्याद्धिंसिते प्रतिहिंसितं
न तत्र दोषं पश्यामि दुष्टे दुष्टं समाचरेत्।।

Kṛte pratikṛtim kuryaaddhimsite pratihimsitam
Na tatra dosham paśyāmi dushṭe dushṭam samaacharet.

## WISE ONES

वैद्यं पानरतं नटं कुपठिनं स्वाध्यायहीनं द्विजं
योधं कापुरुषं हयं गतरयं मूर्खं परिव्राजकं
राजानं च कुमन्त्रिभिः परिवृतं देशं च सोपद्रवं
भार्यां यौवनगर्वितां पररतां मुञ्चन्ति ते पण्डिताः।।

Vaidyam paanaratam naṭam kupaṭhinam svaadhyāy-aheenam dvijam
Yodham kaapurusham hayam gatarayam moorkham parivraajakam
Raajaanam cha kumantribhiḥ parivṛtam deśam cha sopadravam
Bhaaryaam yauvanagarvitaam pararataam muñchanti te paṇḍitaaḥ.

## WICKED ONES

Do unto others as they do unto you,
If someone tries to kill you, return the favour,
I do not see anything wrong in this,
Wicked persons should be dealt with wickedly.

## WISE ONES

They are wise, who give up:
the physician, addicted to drinking,
the actor who cannot read his lines correctly,
the Brahmin who has not studied the Vedas,
the unmanly warrior,
the steed without speed,
the foolish sage,
the ruler, surrounded by bad counsellors,
the troubled country,
and the wife arrogant about her youth and interested in others.

# PART TWO

# WONDROUS WHISPERS OF WISDOM FROM HITOPADESA

## WONDROUS WHISPERS OF WISDOM FROM HITOPADESA

## ACTION

शास्त्राण्यधीत्यापि भवन्ति मूढ़ाः
यस्तु क्रियावान् पुरुषः स विद्वान्
सुचिन्तितं चौषधमातुराणां
न नाममात्रेण करोत्यरोगं।।

Śaastrāṇyadheetyaapi bhavanti mooḍhaaḥ
Yastu kriyaavaan purushaḥ sa vidwaan
Suchintitam chaushadhamaaturaaṇaam
Na naamamaatreṇa karotyarogam.

## AFFECTION

मुखं प्रसन्नं विमला च दृष्टिः
कथानुरागो मधुरा च वाणी
स्नेहोऽधिकः संभ्रमदर्शनं च
सदानुरक्तस्य नरस्य चिह्नं।।

Mukham prasannam vimalaa cha dṛshṭiḥ
Kathaanuraago madhuraa cha vāṇee
Snehoadhikaḥ sambhramadarśanam cha
Sadaanuraktasya narasya chihnam.

## ASSOCIATION

हीयते हि मतिस्तात हीनैः सह समागमात्
समैश्च समतामेति विशिष्टैश्च विशिष्यते।।

Heeyate hi matistaata heenaiḥ saha samaagamaat
Samaiścha samataameti viśishṭaiścha viśishyate.

कीडोपि सुमनः संगादारोहति सतां शिरः
अश्मापि याति देवत्वं महद्भिः सुप्रतिष्ठितः।।

Keeḍopi sumanaḥ sangaadaarohati sataam śiraḥ
Aśmaapi yaati devatvam mahadbhiḥ supratishṭhitaḥ.

## ACTION

Even after studying various sciences, some remain fools,
He is the wise one, who can act,
Well prescribed medicines have to be taken by patients,
By mere mention of a medicine's name, a disease is not cured.

## AFFECTION

The affectionate one's signs are:
A pleasing face, clear eyes,
interest in telling good stories, sweet speech, total sincerity, hearty reception when we meet.

## ASSOCIATION

Child, the mind, gets bad by association with evil persons,
it remains the same, by association with persons who are neither good nor bad,
by association with high quality persons, it shines.

Even the worm gets on the heads of the elite, by its association with flowers.
Even a stone, when set up by the great, attains divine stature.

अश्वः शस्त्रं शास्त्रं वीणा वाणी नरश्च नारी च
पुरुषविशेषं प्राप्य भवन्ति योग्या अयोग्याश्च।।

Aśvaḥ śastram śaastram veeṇaa vāṇee naraścha naaree cha
Purushaviśesham praapya bhavanti yogyaa ayogyaaścha.

## BEAUTY

किमप्यस्ति स्वभावेन सुन्दरं वाप्यसुन्दरं
यदेव रोचते यस्मै भवेत्तत्तस्य सुन्दरं।।

Kimapyasti svabhaavena sundaram vaapyasundaram
Yadeva rochate yasmai bhavettattasya sundaram.

## CAPTIVATION

लुब्धमर्थेन गृह्णीयात् क्रुद्धमञ्जलिकर्मणा
मूर्खं धर्म्मानुवृत्या च तत्वार्थेन च पण्डितं।।

Lubdhamarthena gṛhṇeeyaat kruddhamañjalikarmaṇaa
Moorkham dharmmaanuvṛtyaa cha tatvaarthena cha paṇḍitam.

## CHARACTER

सर्वस्य हि परीक्ष्यन्ते स्वभावा नेतरेगुणाः
अतीत्य हि गुणान् सर्वान् स्वभावो मूर्ध्नि वर्तते।।

Sarvasya hi pareekshyante svabhaavaa netareguṇaaḥ
Ateetya hi guṇaan sarvaan svabhaavo moordhni vartate.

Horse, weapon, learning, the lute, word, man, woman—these become good or bad according to the person to whom they are yoked.

## BEAUTY

There is nothing intrinsically beautiful or not beautiful,
Whatever appeals to one becomes beautiful, otherwise not.

## CAPTIVATION

The greedy can be captivated with money,
the angry one by bowing down,
the fool by allowing freedom of action,
and the intellectual by philosophy.

## CHARACTER

The main thing to be tested in all people is character,
not other qualities.
Character stays at the top, transcending all other qualities.

## DISCRETION

वरं मौनं कार्यं न च वचनमुक्तं यदनृतं
वरं क्लैब्यं पुंसां न च परकळत्राभिगमनं
वरं प्राणत्यागो न च पिशुन वाक्येष्वभिरुचिः
वरं भिक्षाशित्वं न च परधनास्वादनसुखं।।

Varam maunam kaaryam na cha vachanamuktam yadanṛtam
Varam klaibyam pumsaam na cha parakaḷatrābhigamanam
Varam praaṇatyaago na cha piśunavaakyeshvabhiruchiḥ
Varam bhikshaaśitvam na cha paradhanaasvaadana-sukham.

## DONATION

दातव्यमितियद्दानं दीयतेऽनुपकारिणे
देशे प्रशस्ते काले च तद्दानं सात्विकं स्मृतं।।

Daatavyamitiyaddaanam deeyateanupakaariṇe
Deśe praśaste kaale cha taddaanam saatvikam smṛtam.

## DOUBT

न संशयमनारुह्य नरो भद्राणि पश्यति
संशयं पुनरारुह्य यदि जीवति पश्यति।।

Na samśayamanaaruhya naro bhadraaṇi paśyati
Samśayam punaraaruhya yadi jeevati paśyati.

## DOWNFALL

आरोप्यते शिला शैले यत्नेन महता सह
निपात्यते क्षणादेव तथात्मा सुखदुःखयोः।।

Aaropyate śilaa śaile yatnena mahataa saha
Nipaatyate kshaṇaadeva tathaatmaa sukhadukhayoḥ.

## DISCRETION

It is better to remain silent, rather than speak untruth,
It is better to be impotent rather than go to others' wives,
It is better to give up life rather than indulge in slander,
It is better to beg rather than enjoy others' wealth.

## DONATION

That donation is the ideal donation which is given without expecting any return, at the right time and place.

## DOUBT

Without doubting or questioning, man cannot attain prosperity,
Finding the answers to the doubts or questions, one lives and perceives the truth.

## DOWNFALL

A rock can be taken up to the mountaintop with great effort,
but it can be thrown down very easily,
so too are the ascent and downfall of a person.

## EVIL ONES

दुर्जनो नार्जवं याति सेव्यमानोऽपि नित्यशः
स्वेदनाभ्यञ्जनोपायैः श्वपुच्छमिव नामितं।।

Durjano naarjavam yaati sevyamaano'pi nityaśaḥ
Svedanaabhyañjanopaayaiḥ śvapucchamiva naamitam.

दुर्जनः प्रियवादी च नैतद्विश्वासकारणं
मधु तिष्ठति जिह्वाग्रे हृदये तु हालाहलं।।

Durjanaḥ priyavaadee cha naitadviśvaasakaaraṇam
Madhu tishṭhati jihvaagre hṛdaye tu haalaahalam.

## FATE

अयाचितः सुखं दत्ते याचितश्च न यच्छति
सर्वस्वं चापि हरते विधिरुच्छृंखलो नृणां।।

Ayaachitaḥ sukham datte yaachitaścha na yacchati
Sarvasvam chaapi harate vidhirucchrunkhalo nṛṇaam.

स हि गगनविहारी कन्मषध्वंसकारी
दशशतकरकारी ज्योतिषां मध्यचारी
विधुरपि विधियोगात् ग्रह्यते राहुणासौ
लिखितमपि ललाटे प्रोज्झितुं कः समर्थः।।

Sa hi gaganaviharee kanmashadhvamsakaaree
Daśaśatakarakaaree jyotishaam madhyachaaree
Vidhurapi vidhiyogaat grahyate raahuṇaasau
Likhitamapi lalaaṭe projjhitum kaḥ samarthaḥ.

## EVIL ONES

Evil persons do not become upright, even if served loyally,
The dog's tail does not become straight, even if sweated or smeared with oil.

The evil one, even if sweetspoken, should not be trusted;
There is honey in the tongue, but poison in the heart.

## FATE

It gives happiness, unasked,
does not give, when asked,
It robs everything,
Fate is fetterless, as far as human beings are concerned.

It moves freely in the sky,
It dispels darkness,
It has myriad rays,
It moves in the midst of stars,
Yet the moon is eclipsed (by Rahu*),
Who is competent in altering the fate written on the forehead?

*The myth in India is that the moon is eclipsed when Rahu, the Dragon, swallows the moon.

## FIGHT

बलिना सह योद्धव्यमिति नास्ति निदर्शनं
प्रतिवातं नहि घनः कदाचिदुपसर्प्पति।।

Balinaa saha yoddhavyamiti naasti nidarśanam
Prativātam nahi ghanaḥ kadaachidupasarppati.

## FRIEND

यस्य मित्रेण संभाषा यस्य मित्रेण संगति
मित्रेण सह यो भुङ्क्ते ततो नास्तीह पुण्यवान्।।

Yasya mitreṇa sambhaashaa yasya mitreṇa samgati
Mitreṇa saha yo bhunkte tato naasteeha puṇyavaan.

स्वाभाविकं तु यन्मित्रं भाग्येनैवोपजायते
तदकृत्रिमसौहाद्र्दमापत्स्वपि न मुञ्चति।।

Svaabhaavikam tu yanmitram bhaagyenaivopajaayate
Tadakritrimasauhaarddamaapatsvapi na muñchati.

मित्रं प्रीतिरसायनं नयनयोरानन्दनं चेतसः
पात्रं यत् सुखदुःखयो सहभवेन्मित्रेण तद्दुर्ल्लभं
ये चान्ये सुहृदः समृद्धिसमये द्रव्याभिला-
षाकुलास्ते सर्वत्र मिलन्ति तत्वनिकषग्रावा तु तेषां विपत्।।

Mitram preetirasaayanam nayanayoraanandanam chetasaḥ
Paatram yat sukhadukhayo sahabhavenmitreṇa taddurllabham
Ye chaanye suhridaḥ samṛddhisamaye dravyaabhila-
ashākulāste sarvatra milanti tatvanikashagrāvā tu teshām vipat.

## FIGHT

Nobody need say: Don't fight with one, superior in strength,
The cloud never moves against the wind!

## FRIEND

He who can converse with friends, mix with friends and eat with friends, who can be more blessed than him?

One gets a true friend only by good fortune,
Such flawless friendship is not given up even in difficulties.

A friend is the magic potion competent to give happiness,
he pleases the eyes and the heart,
he shares both pleasure and pain equally
The pleasure of being with a friend cannot be got anywhere else,
One can find everywhere companions who are only after your money,
The whetstone to test friends is difficulties and discerning wisdom.

## FRUITFULNESS

अञ्जनस्य क्षयं दृष्ट्वा वल्मीकस्य च सञ्चयं
अवन्ध्यं दिवसं कुर्याद्दानाध्ययन कर्मसु।।

Añjanasya kshayam dṛshṭvaa valmeekasya cha sañchayam
Avandhyam divasam kuryaaddaanaadhyayana karmasu.

सुजीर्णमन्नं सुविचक्षणः सुतः
सुशासिता स्त्री नृपतिः सुसेवितः
सुचिन्त्यचोक्तं सुविचार्य यत् कृतं
सुदीर्घकालेऽपि न यान्ति विक्रियां।।

Sujeerṇamannam suvichakshaṇaḥ sutaḥ
Suśaasitaa stree nṛpatiḥ susevitaḥ
Suchintyachoktam suvichaarya yat kṛtam
Sudeerghakaale api na yaanti vikriyaam.

## GOAL

नाद्रव्ये निहिता काचित् क्रिया गुणवती भवेत्
न व्यापारशतेनापि शुकवत् पाठ्यते बकः।।

Naadravye nihitaa kaachit kriyaa guṇavatee bhavet
Na vyaapaaraśatenaapi śukavat paaṭhyate bakaḥ.

## GOD

अचिन्तितानि दुःखानि यथैवायान्ति देहिनां
सुखान्यपि तथा मन्ये दैवमत्रातिरिच्यते।।

Achintitaani dukhaani yathaivaayaanti dehinaam
Sukhaanyapi tathaa manye daivamatraatirichyate.

## FRUITFULNESS

See the collyrium fade away and the anthill grow and make fruitful the day with donation and study.

Well digested food, responsible son,
well trained woman, well served ruler,
the word spoken after deep deliberation,
the well planned deed,
all these, in the long run, will not be fruitless.

## GOAL

A deed done for an inappropriate goal cannot give results, Even with a hundred efforts, a crane cannot speak like a parrot.

## GOD

Just as unexpected sorrows come to people,
so too come pleasures.
I think everything happens according to the will of God.

अरक्षितं तिष्ठति दैवरक्षितं
सुरक्षितं दैवहतं विनश्यति
जीवत्यनाथोऽपि वने विसर्जितः
कृतप्रयत्नोपि गृहे न जीवति।।

Arakshitam tishṭhati daivarakshitam
Surakshitam daivahatam vinaśyati
Jeevatyanaatho'pi vane visarjitaḥ
Kṛtaprayatnopi gṛhe na jeevati.

येन शुक्लीकृता हंसाः शुकाश्च हरितीकृताः
मयूराश्चित्रिता येन स ते वृत्तिं विधास्यति।।

Yena śukleekritaa hamsaaḥ śukaaścha hariteekritaaḥ
Mayooraaśchitritaa yena sa te vṛttim vidhaasyati.

यथाह्येकेन चक्रेण न रथस्य गतिर्भवेत्
एवं पुरुषकारेण विना दैवं न सिद्ध्यति।।

Yathaahyekena chakreṇa na rathasya gatirbhavet
Evam purushakaareṇa vinaa daivam na siddhyati.

## GOOD COMPANY

संसार कटुवृक्षस्य द्वे फले ह्यमृतोपमे
सुभाषित रसास्वादः संगति सुजने जने।।

Samsaara kaṭuvrikshasya dve phale hyamritopame
Subhaashita rasaasvaadaḥ samgati sujane jane.

## GOOD ONES

साधो प्रकोपितस्यापि मनो नायान्ति विक्रियां
नहि तापयितुं शक्यं सागराम्भस्तृणोर्णया।।

Saadho prakopitasyaapi mano naayaanti vikriyaam
Nahi taapayitum śakyam saagaraambhastriṇorṇayaa.

The unprotected, if protected by God, survive.
Even the well protected perish, if willed by God.
The orphan deserted in the jungle lives,
While the one brought up with care in the house dies.

He who has made the swans white, the parrots green, and the peacocks multicoloured, will give you too a means of livelihood.

Just as the chariot cannot move on one wheel,
without man, God cannot achieve anything.

## GOOD COMPANY

The bitter tree of Samsara has two nectarlike fruits:
(They are) enjoyment of good sayings and the company of good persons.

## GOOD ONES

Even if something is done to provoke their anger, good persons do not have any mental disturbance, The waters of the ocean cannot be heated up by throwing lit up grass into them.

नारिकेळफलाकाराः दृश्यन्तेऽपि हि सज्जनाः
अन्ये बदरिकाकाराः बहिरेव मनोहराः।।

Naarikeḷaphalaakaaraaḥ driśyante api hi sajjanaaḥ
Anye badarikaakaaraaḥ bahireva manoharaaḥ.

सन्त एव सतां नित्यमापदुद्धरणक्षमाः
गजानां पङ्कमग्नानां गजाः एव धुरन्धराः।।

Santa eva sataam nityamaapaduddharaṇakshamaaḥ
Gajaanaam pankamagnaanaam gajaaḥ eva dhurandharaaḥ.

## GOOD QUALITIES

सर्वहिंसानिवृत्ताः ये नराः सर्वसहाश्च ये
सर्वस्याश्रयभूताश्च ते नराः स्वर्गगामिनः।।

Sarvahimsaanivrittaaḥ ye naraaḥ sarvasahaaścha ye
Sarvasyaaśrayabhootaaścha te naraaḥ svargagaaminaḥ.

सत्यं शौर्यं दया त्यागो नृपस्यैते महागुणाः
एभिर्मुक्तो महीपालः प्राप्नोति खलु वाच्यतां।।

Satyam śauryam dayaa tyaago nṛpasyaite mahaaguṇaaḥ
Ebhirmukto maheepaalaḥ praapnoti khalu vaachyataam.

## GREAT ONES

आमरणान्ताः प्रणयाः कोपास्तत्क्षण भंगुराः
परित्यागाश्च निस्संगाः भवन्ति हि महात्मनां।।

Aamaraṇaantaaḥ praṇayaaḥ kopaastatkshaṇa bhanguraaḥ
Parityaagaaścha nissangaaḥ bhavanti hi mahaatmanaam.

Good persons are seen to be like coconuts (not very attractive externally, but full of stuff inside).
Others are like the red fruit of the jujube tree (attractive only externally).

Only good ones are competent in saving good ones from danger,
Only elephants are competent in bringing out mired elephants.

## GOOD QUALITIES

Those who refrain from all violence, tolerate everything, and give refuge to everyone, are fit to go to heaven!

Truthfulness, courage, kindness and sacrifice are the most important qualities of a Ruler.
A Ruler devoid of these qualities becomes the object of disrepute.

## GREAT ONES

The affections of great ones last till death,
Their anger is dispelled in a moment,
Their sacrifices are totally detached.

## GREED

सुमहन्त्यपि शास्त्राणि धारयन्तो बहुश्रुताः
च्छेत्तारः संशयानां च क्लिश्यन्ते लोभमोहिताः।।

Sumahantyapi śaastraaṇi dhaarayanto bahuśrutaaḥ
Cchettaaraḥ samśayaanaam cha kliśyante lobhamohitaaḥ.

## HAPPINESS

अर्थागमो नित्यमरोगिता च
प्रिया च भार्या, प्रियवादिनी च
वश्यश्च पुत्रोऽर्थकारी च विद्या
शड्जीवलोकेषु सुखानि राजन्।।

Arthaagamo nityamarogitaa cha
Priyaa cha bhaaryaa priyavaadinee cha
Vaśyaścha putroarthakaaree cha vidyaa
Śaḍjeevalokeshu sukhaani raajan.

विषलिप्तस्य भक्तस्य दन्तस्य चलितस्य च
अमात्यस्य च दुष्टस्य मूलादुद्धरणं सुखं।।

Vishaliptasya bhaktasya dantasya chalitasya cha
Amātyasya cha dushṭasya moolaaduddharaṇam sukham.

## HELP

श्लाघ्यः स एको भुवि मानवानां
स उत्तमः सत्पुरुषः स धन्यः
यस्यार्थिनो वा शरणागतो वा
नाशाभिभंगाद्विमुखाः प्रयान्ति।।

Ślaaghyaḥ sa eko bhuvi maanavaanaam
Sa uttamaḥ satpurushaḥ sa dhanyaḥ
Yasyaarthino vaa śaraṇaagato vaa
Naaśaabhibhangaadvimukhaaḥ prayaanti.

## GREED

Even those who have mastered learned sciences and can dispel doubts and are intellectuals come to grief, falling a prey to greed.

## HAPPINESS

In this worldly life there are six means to happiness:
Incoming riches every day,
physical health,
dear and sweetspoken spouse,
obedient progeny,
and productive learning.

Rooting out poisoned food, a moving tooth, and a wicked counsellor gives happiness.

## HELP

In this world, he is praiseworthy, he is blessed, he is the superior one, the good one,
to whom people come seeking help or refuge and do not go away disappointed.

## HERO

को वीरस्य मनस्विनः स्वविषयः किं वा विदेशस्तथा
यं देशं श्रयते तमेव कुरुते बाहुप्रतापार्जितं
य द्दंष्ट्रानखलांगलप्रहरणैः सिंहो वनं गाहते
तस्मिन्नेव हतद्विपेन्द्ररुधिरैस्तृष्णां छिनत्यात्मनः।।

Ko veerasya manasvinaḥ svavishayaḥ kim vaa videśastathaa
Yam ddeśam śrayate tameva kurute baahuprataapaarjitam
Ya ddamshtraanakhalaangalapraharaṇaiḥ simho vanam gaahate
Tasminneva hatadvipendrarudhiraistṛshṇaam cchinatyaatmanaḥ.

मनस्वी म्रियते कामं कार्पण्यं न तु गच्छति
अपि निर्वाणमायाति नानलो याति शीततां।।

Manasvee mriyate kaamam kaarpaṇyam na tu gacchati
Api nirvaaṇamaayaati naanalo yaati śeetataam.

सर्व एव जनः शूरो ह्यनासादितविग्रहः
अदृष्टपरसामर्थ्यः सदर्प्पः को भवेन्नहि।।

Sarva eva janaḥ śooro hyanaasaaditavigrahaḥ
Adṛshṭaparasaamarthyaḥ sadarppaḥ ko bhavennahi.

## HUMAN ANIMAL

अहितहितविचारशून्यबुद्धेः
श्रुतिसमयैर्बहुभिस्तिरस्कृत्य
उदरभरणमात्रकेवलेच्छोः
पुरुषपशोश्च पशोश्च को विशेषः।।

Ahitahitavichaaraśoonyabuddheḥ
Śrutisamayairbahubhistiraskṛtya
Udarabharaṇamaatrakevalecchoḥ
Purushapaśośca paśośca ko viśeshaḥ.

## HERO

To the heroic one what is a native country or a foreign country?
Whatever country he reaches, he makes his own by his valour, as the lion, which enters the jungle and quenches its thirst with the blood of the huge elephants it kills hitting them with its teeth and nails.

The steadyminded hero may die, but will never attain a pitiable weakened state,
The fire may be put out, but it never becomes cold.

All are heroes, who have not faced a battle,
Everyone who has not understood another's capacity is arrogant.

## HUMAN ANIMAL

What is the difference between an animal and the human animal who is not conscious of what is good and what is bad, who is devoid of truthfulness and scriptural awareness and who ever thinks only of filling his belly.

## INERTIA

दोषभीतेरनारम्भस्तत् कापुरुषलक्षणं
कैरजीर्णभयात् प्रातर्भोजनं परिहीयते।।

Doshabheeteranaarambhastat kaapurushalakshaṇam
Kairajeerṇabhayaat praatarbhojanam pariheeyate.

## INTELLECT

उदीरितोऽर्थः पशुनापि गृह्यते
हयाश्च नागाश्च भवन्ति देशिकाः
अनुकतमप्यूह्यति पण्डितो जनः
परेंगितज्ञानफला हि बुद्धयः।।

Udeeritoarthaḥ paśunaapi gṛhyate
Hayaaścha naagaaścha bhavanti deśikaaḥ
Anukatamapyoohyati paṇḍito janaḥ
Parengitajñaanaphalaa hi buddhayaḥ.

असंभवं हेममृगस्य जन्म
तथापि रामो लुलुभे मृगाय
प्रायः समापन्नविपत्तिकाले
धियोऽपि पुंसां मलिनीभवन्ति।।

Asambhavam hemamṛgasya janma
Tathaapi raamo lulubhe mṛgaaya
Praayaḥ samaapannavipattikaale
Dhiyoapi pumsaam malineebhavanti.

## KARMA

रोगशोकपरीताप बन्धन व्यसनानि च
आत्मापराधवृक्षाणां फलान्येतानि देहिनां।।

Rogaśokaparitaapa bandhana vyasanaani cha
Aatmaaparaadhavrikshaaṇaam phalaanyetaani dehinaam.

## INERTIA

Not to start a project out of fear of failure is a ṣign of unmanliness!
Who would ever forgo a breakfast, fearing indigestion?

## INTELLECT

Something made understandable is understood even by animals,
Horses and elephants act according to instructions,
Wise persons discern even unspoken things,
Intellect is intended to understand others' intentions.

The birth of a golden deer is impossible,
Yet Rama wanted to get it,
Usually, when dangers are imminent,
Men's intellects get clouded.

## KARMA

Disease, sorrow, affliction, imprisonment and difficulties—all these are the fruits of the trees of sins committed by human beings themselves.

## LEARNING

अनेकसंशयोच्छेदि परोक्षार्थस्य दर्शकं
सर्वस्य लोचनं शास्त्रं यस्य नास्त्यन्ध एव सः।।

Anekasamśayocchedi parokshaarthasya darśakam
Sarvasya lochanam śaastram yasya naastyandha eva saḥ.

विद्या शस्त्रस्य शास्त्रस्य द्वे विद्ये प्रतिपत्तये
आद्या हासाय वृद्धत्वे द्वितीयाद्रीयते सदा।।

Vidyaa śastrasya śaastrasya dve vidye pratipattaye
Aadyaa haasaaya vṛddhatve dviteeyaadreeyate sadaa.

यत्र विद्वज्जनो नास्ति श्लाघ्यस्तत्राल्पधीरपि
निरस्तपादपे देशे एरण्डोपि द्रुमायते।।

Yatra vidvajjano naasti ślaaghyastatraalpadheerapi
Nirastapaadape deśe eraṇḍopi drumaayate.

## LUSTRE

बलवानपि निस्तेजा कस्य नाभिभवास्पदं
निःशंकं दीयते लोकैः पश्य भस्मचये पदं।।

Balavaanapi nistejaa kasya naabhibhavaaspadam
Niḥśankam deeyate lokaiḥ paśya bhasmachaye padam.

## LEARNING

He is blind, who does not have the knowledge of scriptures which clear many doubts, make patent latent truths and act like an eye for everything.

Weaponry and scriptures are both fit to be learnt.
However, the first leads to ridicule in old age,
the second is always respected.

Where there are no learned intellectuals, even the small minds are praised,
In places where there are no trees, even the castor plant is deemed a tree.

## LUSTRE

The strong, if lustreless, cannot be the basis for victory,
Look! People set their feet in ashes without any concern.

## MIGHT

तृणानि नोन्मूलयति प्रभञ्जनो
मृदूनि नीचैः प्रणतानि सर्वतः
समुच्छ्रितानेव तरून् प्रबाधते
महान् महत्येव करोति विक्रमं।।

Tṛṇaani nonmoolayati prabhañjano
Mṛdooni neechaiḥ praṇataani sarvataḥ
Samucchritaaneva taroon prabaadhate
Mahaan mahatyeva karoti vikramam.

## MONEY

न नरस्य नरो दासो दासश्चार्थस्य सर्वदा
गौरवं लाघवं चापि धनाधननिबन्धनं।।

Na narasya naro daaso daasaśchaarthasya sarvadaa
Gauravam laaghavam chaapi dhanaadhananibandhanam.

जनयन्त्यार्जने दुःखं तापयन्ति विपत्तिषु
मोहयन्ति च सम्पत्तौ कथमर्थाः सुखावहाः।।

Janayantyaarjane dukham taapayanti vipattishu
Mohayanti cha sampattau kathamarthaaḥ sukhaavahaaḥ.

दरिद्रान् भर कौन्तेय मा प्रयच्छेश्वरे धनं
व्याधितस्यौषधं पथ्यं नीरुजस्य किमौषधैः।।

Daridraan bhara kaunteya maa prayaccheśvare dhanam
Vyaadhitasyaushadham pathyam neerujasya kimaushadhaiḥ.

## MIGHT

The wind does not destroy the soft, ever bending grass,
It only affects the tall trees,
The mighty one shows his might only against the mighty.

## MONEY

No man is slave of another man; man is always the slave of money;
Respect or contempt is entirely dependent on money or the lack of it.

It creates sorrow in earning it,
causes trouble in difficulties,
drives into delusion for riches,
How can money give happiness?

Protect the poor,
Do not give money to the rich,
Medicine is apt for the sick,
What is the use of medicine for the healthy?

तानीन्द्रियाण्यविकलानि तदेव नाम
सा बुद्धिरप्रतिहता वचनं तथैव
अर्थोष्मणा विरहितः पुरुषः क्षणेन
सोऽप्यन्य एव भवतीति विचित्रमेतत्।।

Taaneendriyaaṇyavikalaani tadeva naama
Saa buddhirapratihataa vachanam tathaiva
Arthoshmaṇaa virahitaḥ purushaḥ kshaṇena
Soapyanya eva bhavateeti vichitrametat.

## PATIENCE

क्षमा शत्रौ च मित्रे च यतीनामेव भूषणं
अपराधिषु सत्वेषु नृपाणां सैव दूषणं।।

Kshamaa śatrau cha mitre cha yateenaameva bhooshaṇam
Aparaadhishu satveshu nṛpaaṇaam saiva dooshaṇam.

## POSSIBILITY

यदशक्यं तच्छक्यं यच्छक्यं शक्यमेव तत्
नोदके शकटं याति न च नौर्गच्छति स्थले।।

Yadaśakyam tacchakyam yacchakyam śakyameva tat
Nodake śakaṭam yaati na cha naurgacchati sthale.

## PRECEPT & PRACTICE

गतानुगतिको लोकः कुट्टिनीमुपदेशिनीं
प्रमाणयति नो धर्मे तथा गोघ्नमपि द्विजं।।

Gataanugatiko lokaḥ kuṭṭineemupadeśineem
Pramaaṇayati no dharme tathaa goghnamapi dvijam.

When a man loses the energy of money, in a moment, his sound senses, his reputation, his unerring intellect, his words all desert him and treat him like an outsider! This is amazing!

## PATIENCE

Patience with friends and enemies is an ornament for sages. It is a flaw for rulers, especially when dealing with those who err.

## POSSIBILITY

What is impossible cannot be done,
What can be done can be done,
The cart cannot move in water,
Nor can a boat move on land.

## PRECEPT & PRACTICE

Though people follow others mindlessly,
No one takes seriously a prostitute preaching ethics,
Nor a brahmin who has killed a cow.

## PREFERENCE

वरं शून्या शाला न च खलु वरो दुष्टवृषभो
वरं वेश्या पत्नी न पुनरविनीता कुलवधूः
वरं वासोऽरण्ये न पुनरविवेकाधिपपुरे
वरं प्राणत्यागो न पुनरधमानामुपगमः।।

Varam śoonyaa śaalaa na cha khalu varo dushṭavṛshabho
Varam veśyaa patnee na punaravineetaa kulavadhooḥ
Varam vaaso araṇye na punaravivekaadhipapure
Varam praaṇatyaago na punaradhamaanaamupagamaḥ.

## PROBLEMS

यौवनं धनसम्पत्तिः प्रभुत्वमविवेकिता
एकैकमप्यनर्थाय किमु यत्र चतुष्टयं।।

Yauvanam dhanasampattiḥ prabhutvamavivekitaa
Ekaikamapyanarthaaya kimu yatra chatushṭayam.

## RARITY

दानं प्रियवाक्सहितं
ज्ञानमगर्वं क्षमान्वितं शौर्यं
वित्तं त्यागनियुक्तं
दुर्लभमेतच्चतुर्भद्रं।।

Daanam priyavaaksahitam
Jñaanamagarvam kshamaanvitam śauryam
Vittam tyaaganiyuktam
Durlabhametacchaturbhadram.

## PREFERENCE

An empty cowshed is better than a bad bull,
A prostitute wife is better than an arrogant family girl,
Residence in the forest is better than in a city under a senseless ruler,
Giving up life is better than seeking refuge in a lowly one.

## PROBLEMS

Youth, affluence, power, lack of discretion
each one of these can cause problems,
what to say if all the four are present in one person?

## RARITY

These four good things are rare:
Donation with sweet words,
knowledge without arrogance,
courage with patience,
and abundance of wealth with a sacrificing tendency.

## RESIDENCE

लोकयात्रा भयं लज्जा दाक्षिण्यं त्यागशीलता
पञ्च यत्र न विद्यन्ते न कुर्यात्तत्र संस्थितं।।

Lokayātraa bhayam lajjaa daakshiṇyam tyaagaśeelatā
Pañcha yatra na vidyante na kuryaattatra samsthitam.

तत्र मित्र न वस्तव्यं यत्र नास्ति चतुष्टयं
ऋणदाता च वैद्यश्च श्रोत्रियः सजला नदी।।

Tatra mitra na vastavyam yatra naasti chatushṭayam
Ṛṇadaataa cha vaidyaścha śrotriyaḥ sajalaa nadee.

## RIGHTEOUSNESS

यस्य धर्मविहीनानि दिनान्यायान्ति यान्ति च
स लोहकारभस्त्रेव श्वसन्नपि न जीवति।।

Yasya dharmaviheenaani dinaanyaayaanti yaanti cha
Sa lohakaarabhasreva śvasannapi na jeevati.

## RULER

राजा कुलवधूर्विप्राः मन्त्रिणश्च पयोधराः
स्थानभ्रष्टाः न शोभन्ते दन्ता केशा नराः नखाः।।

Raajā kulavadhoorvipraaḥ mantriṇaścha payodharaaḥ
Sthaanabhrashṭaaḥ na śobhante dantaa keśaa naraaḥ nakhaaḥ.

## RESIDENCE

One should not reside where these five are absent: Conveniences for living, fear, modesty, generosity and sacrificial nature.

Friend, do not stay in a place where four things are missing: The moneylender, doctor, priest and a river full of water.

## RIGHTEOUSNESS

He, whose days pass without righteous deeds,
though breathing, does not live,
like the blower of the metal worker.

## RULER

The Ruler is like the family bride!
Intellectuals and counsellors are the breasts, the people are the teeth, hair and nails,
The Ruler does not shine, if any of these are out of place (displaced).

सत्यानृता च परुषा प्रियवादिनी च
हिंस्रा दयालुरपि चार्थपरा वदान्या
नित्यव्यया प्रचुररत्नधनागमा च
वारांगनेव नृपनीतिरनेकरूपा।।

Satyaanṛtaa cha parushaa priyavaadinee cha
Himsraa dayaalurapi chaarthaparaa vadaanyaa
Nityavyayaa prachuraratnadhanaagamaa cha
Vaaraanganeva nṛpaneetiranekaroopaa.

## SATISFACTION

न योजनशतं दूरं बध्यमानस्य तृष्णया
सन्तुष्टस्य करप्राप्तेप्यर्थ भवति नादरः।।

Na yojanaśatam dooram badhyamaanasya tṛshṇayaa
Santushṭasya karapraaptepyartha bhavati naadaraḥ.

## SAVING

आपदर्थं धनं रक्षेद्दारान् रक्षेद्धनैरपि
आत्मानं सततं रक्षेद्दारैरपि धनैरपि।।

Aapadartham dhanam raksheddaaraan raksheddhanairapi
Aatmaanam satatam raksheddaarairapi dhanairapi.

## SERVANT

प्रणमत्युन्नतिहेतोर्
जीवितहेतोर् विमुञ्चति प्राणान्
दुःखीयति सुखहेतोः
को मूढः सेवकादन्यः।।

Praṇamatyunnatihetor
Jeevitahetor vimuñchati prāṇaan
Dukheeyati sukhahetoḥ
Ko mooḍhaḥ sevakaadanyaḥ.

A ruler's policy is multifaceted like a prostitute:
Speak untruth as well as truth,
Speak harshly and sweetly,
Be punitive as also compassionate,
Give importance to money, but also be generously giving,
Be a spendthrift, at the same time, amass wealth.

## SATISFACTION

To one driven by desire, a hundred miles is no distance,
To the satisfied, there is no allure even in riches come to hand.

## SAVING

Wealth should be saved for emergencies,
Wife should be saved more than money,
Self should be saved always, above wife or wealth.

## SERVANT

He bows down desiring to rise,
gives up life in order to live,
suffers sorrow desiring happiness,
Who is more foolish than a servant?

## SON

कोऽर्थः पुत्रेण जातेन यो विद्वान् न च धार्मिकः
काणेन चक्षुषा किं वा चक्षुः पीडैव केवलं।।

Ko arthaḥ putreṇa jaatena yo vidwaan na cha dhaarmikaḥ
Kaaṇena chakshushaa kim vaa chakshuḥ peeḍaiva kevalam.

वरमेको गुणी पुत्रो न च मूर्खशतान्यपि
एकश्चन्द्रस्तमो हन्ति न च तारागणः क्वचित्।।

Varameko guṇee putro na cha moorkhaśataanyapi
Ekaśchandrastamo hanti na cha taaraagaṇaḥ kvachit.

निरुत्साहं निरानन्दं निर्वीर्यमरिनन्दनं
मा स्म सीमन्तिनी काचिज्जनयेत् पुत्रमीदृशं।।

Nirutsaaham niraanandam nirveeryamarinandanam
Maa sma seemantinee kaachijjanayet putrameedriśam.

## TRANSIENCE

जलान्तश्चन्द्रचपलं जीवितं खलु देहिनां
तथाविधमिति ज्ञात्वा शश्वत् कल्याणमाचरेत्।।

Jalaantaśchandrachapalam jeevitam khalu dehinaam
Tathaavidhamiti jñaatvaa śaśvat kalyaaṇamaacharet.

## TRUST

नदीनां शस्त्रपाणिनां नखिनां शृङ्गिनां तथा
विश्वासो नैव कर्तव्यः स्त्रीषु राजकुलेषु च।।

Nadeenaam śastrapaaṇinaam nakhinaam śṛṅginaam tathaa
Viśvaaso naiva kartavyaḥ streeshu raajakuleshu cha.

## SON

What is the use of a son born, who is neither learned nor righteous?
What is the use of a diseased eye? Merely pain in the eye!

One son with good qualities is better than a hundred foolish ones.
One moon dispels darkness, not a myriad stars.

Let not any woman give birth to a son, who has no zeal, no happy disposition, no valour and who pleases the enemies.

## TRANSIENCE

Life of human beings is as transient as the moon's reflection in water.
Realising this, good deeds should be done always.

## TRUST

Rivers, armed ones, animals with claws and horns, women and ruling families should never be trusted.

## UNION, UNITY

संहति श्रेयसी पुंसां स्वकुलैरल्पकैरपि
तुषेणापि परित्यक्ता न प्ररोहन्ति तण्डुलाः।।

Samhati śreyasee pumsaam svakulairalpakairapi
Tusheṇaapi parityaktaa na prarohanti taṇḍulaaḥ.

अल्पानामपि वस्तुनां संहतिः कार्यसाधिका
तृणैर्गुणत्वमापन्नैर्बध्यन्ते मत्तदन्तिनः।।

Alpaanaamapi vastunaam samhatiḥ kaaryasaadhikaa
Tṛṇairguṇatvamaapannairbadhyante mattadantinaḥ.

## WEALTH

निजसौख्यं निरुन्धानो यो धनार्जनमिच्छति
परार्थभारवाहीव क्लेशस्यैव हि भाजनं।।

Nijasaukhyam nirundhaano yo dhanaarjanamicchati
Paraarthabhaaravāheeva kleśasyaiva hi bhaajanam.

## WISE ONES

अजरामरवत् प्राज्ञो विद्यामर्थं च साधयेत्
गृहीत इव केशेषु मृत्युना धर्ममाचरेत्।।

Ajaraamaravat praajño vidyaamartham cha saadhayet
Gṛheeta iva keśeshu mṛtyunaa dharmamaacharet.

काव्यशास्त्रविनोदेन कालो गच्छति धीमताम्
व्यसनेन च मूर्खाणां निद्रया कलहेन वा।।

Kaavyaśaastravinodena kaalo gacchati dheemataam
Vyasanena cha moorkhaaṇaam nidrayaa kalahena vaa.

## UNION, UNITY

It is good if people of one family stay together, even if they are weak,
Even if the chaff gets separated, the grain loses its power to sprout.

Union of even small things can accomplish tasks.
Grass transformed into ropes can bind wild elephants.

## WEALTH

He who wishes to amass wealth, endangering own happiness, becomes the receptacle of sorrow,
like the one who carries burdens for others.

## WISE ONES

The wise one will amass learning and wealth, as if one will not get old or die,
He will however do righteous deeds, as if he is ever held by the hair in grip by death.

Wise men spend their time enjoying the arts and the sciences,
Fools spend their time in bad habits, sleep and quarrels.

# PART THREE

# WONDROUS WHISPERS OF WISDOM FROM TIRUKKURAL

## WONDROUS WHISPERS OF WISDOM FROM TIRUKKURAL

## ACHIEVEMENT

चेयर्करिय चेय्वार् पेरियर् चिरियर्
चेयर्करिय चेय्कलातार्।।

Cheyarkariya cheyvaar periyar chiriyar
Cheyarkariya cheykalaataar.

## ADORNMENT

पणिवुटैयन् इन्चोलन् आतल् ओरुवर्कु
अणियल्ल मट्ट्रुंपिर।।

Paṇivuṭaiyan incholan aatal oruvarku

Aṇiyalla maṭṭṛumpira.

## ALCOHOLISM

ईन्ऱाळ् मुकत्तेयुं इन्नाताल् एन्मट्ट्रुच्
चान्ऱोर् मुखत्तुक्कळि।।

Eenraaḷ mukatteyum innaataal enmaṭṭṛu
Cchaanror mukhattukkaḷi.

## ANGER

चिनमेन्नुं चेन्तारैक्कोल्लि इनमेन्नुं
एमप्पुणैयै चुटुं।।

Chinamennum cherntaaraikkolli inamennum
Emappuṇaiyai chuṭum.

## ACHIEVEMENT

They who achieve seemingly impossible tasks, are the great ones,
Those who cannot, are the small ones.

## ADORNMENT

Being humble and sweetspoken is not only an adornment, many good things result therefrom.

## ALCOHOLISM

Even an indulgent mother cannot bear to see an alcoholic son, what about others?

## ANGER

The fire of anger destroys not only those who are angry, but also their kith and kin, who are his protective canoe.

## BIRTH

उऱङ्कुवतु पोलुं चाक्काटु उरङ्कि
विऴिप्पतु पोलुं पिऱप्पु।।

Urangkuvatu polum chaakkaaṭu uranki
Vizhippatu polum piṛappu.

## CHILDREN

कुऴलिनितु याऴ्इनितु एन्पदं मक्कळ्
मऴलैच्चोल् केळादवर्।।

Kuzhalinitu yaazh initu enpadam makkaḷ
Mazhalaicchol keḷaadavar.

## COMPASSION

अऱुळिल्लाक्र्कु अव्वुलकं इल्लै
पोऱुळिल्लाक्र्कु इव्वुलकं इल्लाकि याङ्कु।।

Aruḷillaarkku avvulakam illai
Poruḷillaarkku ivvulakam illāki yaanku.

पेराण्मै एन्प तऱुकण् ओन्ऱुट्ट्रक्काल्
ऊराण्मै मट्ट्रतन् एकु।।

Peraaṇmai enpa tarukaṇ onruṭṭrakkaal
Ooraaṇmai maṭṭratan eku.

## DEATH

उऱङ्कुवतु पोलुं चाक्काटु उरङ्कि
विऴिप्पतु पोलुं पिरप्पु।।

Urangkuvatu polum chaakkaaṭu uranki
Vizhippatu polum pirappu.

## BIRTH

Death is like sleep; birth is like waking up.

## CHILDREN

They will say: "The flute is sweet, the lute is sweet!", who have not heard the lispings of their kids.

## COMPASSION

Heaven is not for those without compassion,
as this world is not for those without wealth.

Fearlessness is no doubt manliness, but showing compassion when the need arises is its cutting edge.

## DEATH

Death is like sleep, birth is like waking up.

## DELIBERATION

एण्णित्तुणिक करुमं तुणिन्तपिन्
एण्णुवं एन्पतु इऴुक्कु।।

Eṇṇittuṇika karumam tuṇintapin
Eṇṇuvam enpatu izhukku.

## DESIRE

अवावेन्प एल्ला उयिर्क्कुं एञ्ञान्रुं
तवा अप्पिरप्पीनुं वित्तु।।

Avaavenpa ellaa uyirkkum ejñaanrum
Tavaa appirappeenum vittu.

## DICHOTOMY

मक्कळे पोल्वर् कयवर् अवर् अन्न
ओप्पारि याङ्कण्डतु इल्।।

Makkaḷe polvar kayavar avar anna
Oppaari yānkaṇḍatu il.

## DIFFICULTY

मतिनुट्प नूलोटु उटैयार्क्कु अतिनुट्पं
यावुळ मुन्निऱ्प्पवै।।

Matinuṭpa nooloṭu uṭaiyaarkku atinuṭpam
Yaavuḷa munnirppavai.

## DELIBERATION

One should embark on an enterprise only after due deliberation,
To start an enterprise and then deliberate about it is a grievous mistake.

## DESIRE

Desire is the seed of all life, at all times.

## DICHOTOMY

In qualities, one may be wicked, but externally may appear to be good. This kind of dichotomy can be seen only in humankind.

## DIFFICULTY

What difficulty will be insurmountable to one armed with a keen intellect and learning?

## DIFFERENTIATION

पिऱ्प्पोक्कुं एल्ला उयिर्क्कुं चिऱ्प्पोव्वा
चेय तोऴिल् वेट्ट्रमै यान्।।

Pirappokkum ellaa uyirkkum chirappovvaa
Cheya tozhil veṭṭrumai yaan.

## DISEASE

नोय्नाटि नोय्मुतल् नाटि अतुतणिक्कुं
वाय्नाटि वाय्प्पच्चेयल्।।

Noynaaṭi noymutal naaṭi atutaṇikkum
Vaaynaaṭi vaayppaccheyal.

## DOING

चोल्लुतल् यार्क्कुं एळितु अरियवां
चोल्लिय वण्णं चेयल्।।

Chollutal yaarkkum eḷitu ariyavaam
Cholliya vaṇṇam cheyal.

## DUTIES

तेन्पुलत्तार् दैवं विरुन्तोक्कल् तानेन्ऱाङ्कु
ऐम्पुलत्ताऱोम्पल् तलै।।

Tenpulattaar daivam viruntokkal taanenraanku
Aimpulattaaṛompal talai.

## DIFFERENTIATION

By birth all are equal,
It is the skill in action that differentiates.

## DISEASE

Treatment of a disease should be undertaken after ascertaining the nature of the disease, what caused it and how best it can be cured.

## DOING

It is easy to talk, but difficult to do what is promised.

## DUTIES

Discharging one's duties to forefathers, God, guests, family members and oneself (in that order) is the most desirable virtue in a householder.

## EATING

मरुन्तेन वेण्डावां याक्कैक्करुतियतु
अट्ट्रतु पोट्ट्रि उणिन्।।

Maruntena veṇḍaavaam yaakkaikkarutiyatu
Aṭṭratu poṭṭri uṇin.

## EFFORT

ऊऴैयुं उप्पक्कं काण्पर् उलैविन्रि
त्ताऴातु उञ्चट्ट्रुपवर्।।

Oozhaiyum uppakkam kaaṇpar ulaivinri
Ttaazhaatu uñchaṭṭrupavar.

## EGO

यान् एनतेन्नुञ्चेरुक्करुप्पान् वानोर्क्
कुयर्न्त उलकं पुकुं।।

Yaan enatennuñcherukkaruppaan vaanork
Kuyarnta ulakam pukum.

## ENEMIES

तोऴुतकैयुळ्ळुं पटैयोटुङ्कुं ओन्नार्
अऴुत कण्णीरुं अनैत्तु।।

Tozhutakaiyuḷḷum paṭaiyoṭunkum onnaar
Azhuta kaṇṇeerum anaittu.

## EATING

There is no need for medicine, if one eats when hungry (that is, when the food previously eaten is totally digested).

## EFFORT

Those who put in tireless effort, can conquer fate.

## EGO

He who cuts asunder egoistic feeling of "I and mine" gets a reputation higher than heaven.

## ENEMIES

When enemies bow with folded hands, there are probably concealed weapons in their hands,
So too, their tears are not trustworthy.

## ENMITY

इळैताक मुळ्मरङ्कोल्क कळैयुनर्
कैकोल्लुं काऴ्त्त इटत्तु।।

Iḷaitaaka muḷmaramkolka kaḷaiyunar
Kaikollum kaazhtta iṭattu.

## ENVOY

इऱुति पयप्पिनुं एञ्चातु इऱैवर्कु
उऱुति पयप्पतां तूतु।।

Iruti payappinum eñchaatu iraivarku
Uruti payappataam tootu.

## ENVY

कोटुप्पतऴुक्करुप्पान् चुट्टुं उटुप्पतू ऊं
उण्पतू ऊं इन्ऱि केटुं।।

Koṭuppatazhukkaruppaan chuṭṭrum uṭuppatoo oom
Uṇpatoo oom inri keṭum.

## FACE

अटुत्ततु काट्टुं पळिङ्कुपोल् नेञ्चं
कटुत्ततु काट्टुं मुखं।।

Aṭuttatu kaaṭṭum paḷinkupol neñcham
Kaṭuttatu kaaṭṭum mukham.

## ENMITY

The thorny plant should be cut when it is tender, young.
If it is allowed to grow into a tree, it will hurt the hands of those who try to cut it.
(So too enmity should be nipped in the bud.)

## ENVOY

The true envoy discharges his duty by his master, even at great risk to his own life.

## ENVY

Those who are envious of giving gifts, will suffer—not only they but their kith and kin as well—from want of food and clothing.

## FACE

Like the mirror that reveals the object before it,
the face will reveal what is in the mind.

**FAMILY**

कुटिचेय्वल् एन्नुं ओरुवर्कुत्तेय्वम्
मटितट्ट्रुत्तान्मुन्तूरुम्।।

Kuṭicheyval ennum oruvarkutteyvam
Maṭitaṭṭruttaanmuntoorum.

**FARMING**

चुऴन्रुं एर्प्पिन्नतु उलकं अतनाल्
उऴन्तुं उऴवे तलै।।

Chuzhanrum erppinnatu ulakam atanaal
Uzhantum uzhave talai.

उऴुतुण्डु वाऴ्वारे वाऴवार् मट्ट्रेल्लां
तोऴुतुण्डु पिन्चेल्पवर्।।

Uzhutuṇḍu vāzhvaare vaazhavaar maṭṭrellām
Tozhutuṇḍu pinchelpavar.

इलं एन्रचै इरुप्पारै क्काणिन्
निलं नन्नुं नल्लाळ् नकुं।।

Ilam enrachai iruppaarai kkaaṇin
Nilam nannum nallaaḷ nakum.

**FAULTS**

एतिलार् कुट्ट्रंपोल् तङ्कुट्ट्रं काण्किर्पिन्
तीतुण्डो मन्नुं उयिर्क्कु।।

Etilaar kuṭṭrampol tankuṭṭram kaaṇkirpin
Teetuṇḍo mannum uyirkku.

## FAMILY

God will come forward to aid one determined to raise the status of his family.

## FARMING

If one looks around, the world cannot survive without farming,
Hence farming, though strenuous, is the best vocation.

Only farmers live, all others are their dependants.

Mother Earth laughs at those lazy ones who complain that there is no means of livelihood.

## FAULTS

If only those who deride others for their faults, realise their own faults, their lives will be free from slander and sorrow.

## FEELING

अऱिविनान् आकुवतुण्डो पिऱित्तिन् नोय्
तन्नोय् पोऱ् पोट्ऱाक्कटै।।

Arivınaan aakuvatuṇḍo piritin noi
Tannoi por poṭṭraakkaṭai.

## FORGIVENESS

कोन्ऱन्न इन्ना चेयिनुं अवऱ्चेय्त
ओन्ऱुनन्ऱुळ्ळक्केटुम्।।

Konranna innaa cheyinum avarcheyta
Onrunanruḷḷakkeṭum.

ओऱुत्ताक्कोरुनाळै इन्पं पोऱुत्ताक्कु
प्पोन्ऱुन्तुणैयुं पुकऴ्।।

Oruttaarkkorunaaḷai inpam poruttaarkku
Pponruntuṇaiyum pukazḥ.

## FRIENDSHIP

अरियवट्ट्रुळेल्लां अरित्ते पेरियारैप्
पेणित्तमराक्कोळल्।।

Ariyavaṭṭruḷellaam arite periyaaraip
Peṇittamaraakkoḷal.

पेय्क्कण्डुं नञ्चुण्डु अमैवर् नयत्तक्क
नागरीकं वेण्डुपवर्।।

Peykkaṇḍum nañchuṇḍu amaivar nayattakka
Naagareekam veṇḍupavar.

## FEELING

What is the use of knowledge, if one cannot feel another's misfortune as one's own and remedy it.

## FORGIVENESS

Even if one does murderous harm, remembering the help given earlier should enable us to forget and forgive.

Punishing someone who has done wrong gives momentary joy for a day, but forgiving gives lifelong satisfaction.

## FRIENDSHIP

The greatest blessing is to find and get the friendship of great ones.

Cultured and compassionate people will be prepared to taste even poison served by their friends.

नविल्तोरुं नूल्नयंपोलुं पयिल्तोरुं
पण्पुटैयाळर् तोटर्पु।।

Naviltorum noolnayampolum payiltorum
Paṇpuṭaiyāḷar toṭarpu.

## GOD

अकरमुतल एऴुत्तेल्लां आदि
भगवन् मुतट्रे उलकु।।

Akaramutala ezhuttellaam aadi
Bhagavan mutaṭre ulaku.

कट्रतनाल् आय पयनेन्कोल् वालऱिवन्
नट्राळ् तोऴा आर् एनिन्।।

Kaṭṭratanaal aaya payanenkol vālarivan
Naṭṭrāḷ tozhaa aar enin.

## GOOD CONDUCT

ओऴुक्कं विऴुप्पन्तरलान् ओऴुक्कं
उयिरिनुं ओम्पप्पटुम्।।

Ozhukkam vizhuppantaralaan ozhukkam
Uyirinum ompappaṭum.

## GOOD COUNTRY

उऱुपचियुं ओवापिणियुं चेऱुपकैयुं
चेरातु इयल्वतु नाटु।।

Urupachiyum ovaapiṇiyum cherupakaiyum
Cheraatu iyalvatu naaṭu.

Just as reading a good book gives pleasure, friendship with good ones gives happiness (as it grows).

## GOD

The letter A is the first among all letters.
So too is God, the first among all lives.

Of what use is the learning of the learned,
if they do not bow to God, who is pure knowledge.

## GOOD CONDUCT

Good conduct gives honour and dignity, hence it should be deemed dearer than life.

## GOOD COUNTRY

That is the good country which does not have famine, epidemics and warring factions.

## GREAT ONES

पणियुमां एन्ऱुं पेरुमै चिऱुमै
अणियुमां तन्नै वियन्तु।।

Paṇiyumaam enrum perumai chirumai
Aṇiyumaam tannai viyantu.

## GUESTS

विरुन्तु पुऱत्तात् तानुण्डल् चावा
मरुन्तेनिनुं वेण्डऱ्पाऱ्ऱन्ऱु।।

Viruntu purattaat taanuṇḍal chaavā
Marunteninum veṇḍarpaarrnṛu.

मोप्पक्कुऴैयुं अनिच्चं मुकन्तिरिन्तु
नोक्ककक्कुऴैयुं विरुन्तु।।

Moppakkuzhaiyum aniccham mukantirintu
Nokkakkuzhaiyum viruntu.

## HEARING

चेल्वत्तुळ् चेल्वं चेविच्चेल्वं अच्चेल्वं
चेल्वत्तुळ् एल्लां तलै।।

Chelvattuḷ chelvam chevicchelvam acchelvam
Chelvattuḷ ellaam talai.

## HELP

इटनिल् परुवत्तुं ओप्पुरविऱ्कोल्काऱ्
कटनरि काट्चियवऱ्।।

Iṭanil paruvattum oppuravirkolkaar
Kaṭanaṛi kaaṭchiyavar.

## GREAT ONES

Great ones are humble,
Small minds sing their own praises.

## GUESTS

When the guest is waiting outside, it is not desirable to eat, even if the food is death-destroying ambrosia.

The *aniccham* flower wilts, when smelt,
so too guests wilt, when stared at with a frown.

## HEARING

The capacity to hear is the asset of assets; it outshines all other assets.

## HELP

The dutiful, discerning ones will not refrain from helping others even in times of penury.

चातलिन् इन्नाततिल्लै इनिततू ऊं
ईतल् इयैयाक्कटै।।

Chaatalin innaatatillai initatoo oom
Eetal iyaiyaakkaṭai.

अट्ट्राक्कोंन्ऱु आट्ट्राततान् चेल्वं मिकनलं
पेट्ट्राळ् तमियळ्मूत्तट्ट्रु।।

Aṭṭraarkkonṛu aaṭṭraataan chelvam mikanalam
Peṭṭraaḷ tamiyaḷmoottaṭṭru.

नच्चप्पटातवन् चेल्वं नटुऊरुळ्
नच्चु मरं पऴुत्तट्टु।।

Nacchappaṭaatavan chelvam naṭuooruḷ
Nacchu maram pazhuttaṭṭru.

इरक्क इरत्तक्कार् काणिन् करप्पिन्
अवर् पऴि तंपऴि अन्ऱु।।

Irakka irattakkaar kaaṇin karappin
Avar pazhi tampazhi anru.

इरप्पारै इल्लायिन् ईरङ्कण्मा ज्ञालं
मरप्पावै चेन्रु वन्तट्ट्रु।।

Irappaarai illaayin eerankaṇmaa jñaalam
Marappaavai chenru vantaṭṭru.

करवातु उवन्तीयुं कण् अन्नार् कण्णुं
इरवामै कोटि उऱुं।।

Karavaatu uvanteeyum kaṇ annār kaṇṇum
Iravaamai koṭi urum.

Death is sorrowful, but a greater sorrow is the inability to aid the needy.

The wealth of one who does not help the needy is like the beauty of a spinster growing old in loneliness.

The wealth of a miser (who does not help anyone) is like the fruit in a poison tree in the centre of the village.

One can request help from those who can help,
If the help is refused, the fault lies on those who refuse, not on those who ask for it.

If there are none who need help and none who give help, the world would be one full of (heartless) puppets.

It is million times better not to seek help from those who are wholeheartedly willing to help.

## HONOUR

मयिऱ्नीप्पिन् वाऴाकवरिमा अन्नाऱ्
उयिऱ् नीप्पऱ् मानं वरिन्।।

Mayirneeppin vaazhaakavarimaa annaar
Uyir neeppar maanam varin.

## HUMANISM

अरंपोलुं कूर्मैयरेनुं मरंपोल्वऱ्
मक्कट्पण्पिल्लातवऱ्।।

Arampolum koormaiyarenum marampolvar
Makkaṭpaṇpillaatavar.

## IGNORANCE

वेण्मैयेनप्पटुवतु यातेनिन् ओण्मै
उटैयं यां एन्नुं चेरुक्कु।।

Veṇmaiyenappaṭuvatu yaatenin oṇmai
Uṭaiyam yaam ennum cherukku.

## INDUSTRY

मुयर्चि तिरुविनै याक्कुं मुयट्ऱिन्मै
इन्मै पुकुत्ति विटुं।।

Muyarchi tiruvinai yaakkum muyaṭṭrinmai
Inmai pukutti viṭum.

## HONOUR

The reindeer, if shorn of its hair, gives up its life,
So too, the proud, shorn of their honour.

## HUMANISM

Even those with the sharpest intellects are like dead wood, if they do not have humanism.

## IGNORANCE

Ignorance is that arrogance which makes us think we know everything.

## INDUSTRY

Industry creates wealth, lack of it poverty.

## JOB

इतनै इतनाल् इवन् मुटिक्कुं नन्ऱायन्तु
अतनै अवन्कण् विटल्।।

Itanai itanaal ivan muṭikkum nanraayntu
Atanai avankaṇ viṭal.

## JUDGEMENT

कुणनाटि कुट्ट्रमुं नाटि अवट्ट्रुळ्
मिकैनाटि मिक्ककोळल्।।

Kuṇanaaṭi kkuṭṭramum naaṭi avaṭṭruḷ
Mikainaaṭi mikkakoḷal.

## KILLING

तन्नुयिर् नीप्पिनुञ्चेय्यर्क तान्पिरि
तिन्नुयिर् नीक्कुं विनै।।

Tannuyir neeppinuñcheyyarka taanpiri
Tinnuyir neekkum vinai.

## KNOWLEDGE

एप्पोरुळ् एत्तन्मैत्तायिनुं अप्पोरुळ्
मेय्प्पोरुळ् काण्पतरिवु।।

Epporuḷ ettanmaittaayinum apporuḷ
Meypporuḷ kaaṇpatarivu.

## JOB

A person should be entrusted to do a job, after assessing how he will go about it.

## JUDGEMENT

One should judge a person after assessing his good and bad qualities and finding out what predominates.

## KILLING

Even if one's life is in danger, one should not take another's life to save it.

## KNOWLEDGE

To get to know the true nature of a thing, whatever be its external appearance, is true knowledge.

## LAUGHTER

इटुक्कण् वरुङ्काल् नकुकः अतनै
अटुत्तूर्वतु अतोप्प तिल्।।

Iṭukkaṇ varunkaal nakukaḥ atanai
Aṭuttoorvatu atoppa til.

## LAZINESS

कुटियेन्नुं कुऩ्ऱाविळक्कं मटियेन्नुं
माचूर मायन्तु केटुं।।

Kuṭiyennum kunraaviḷakkam maṭiyennum
Maachoora maayntu keṭum.

## LEARNING

कर्क कचटऱक्कर्पवै कट्ट्रपिन्
निर्क अतर्कुत्तक।।

Karka kachaṭarakkarpavai kaṭṭrapin
Nirka atarkuttaka.

## LIE

पोय्मैयुं वाय्मैयिटत्त पुऱैतीर्न्त
नन्मै पयक्कुमेनिन्।।

Poymaiyum vaaymaiyiṭatta puraiteernta
Nanmai payakkumenin.

## LAUGHTER

Laugh at your troubles, that is the best way to get rid of them.

## LAZINESS

Laziness will put out the lustrous lamp of family name.

## LEARNING

One should acquire learning to rectify one's faults.
After learning, one should act according to what has been learnt.

## LIE

Even a lie spoken to cause unmitigated good will be deemed truth.

## LIVING

वैयत्तुळ् वाऴ्वाङ्कु वाऴ्पवन् वान्उऱैयुं
दैय्वत्तुळ् वैक्कप्पटुम्।।

Vaiyattuḷ vaazhvānku vaazhpavan vaan uraiyum
Daiyvattuḷ vaikkappaṭum.

## LOVE

अन्पीनुं आऱ्वं उटैमै अतु ईनुं
नण्पेन्नुं नाटाच्चिऱप्पु।।

Anpeenum ārvam uṭaimai atu eenum
Naṇpennum nāṭaacchirappu.

## LUST

पिऱन्मनै नोक्कात पेरानमै चान्ऱोर्कु
कऱनोन्ऱो आन्ऱवोऴुक्कु।।

Piranmanai nokkaata peraanmai chaanrorku
Karanonro aanravozhukku.

## MASKS

पुऱङ्कुन्ऱि कण्टनैयरेनुं अकङ्कुन्ऱि
मूक्किऱ् करियार् उटैत्तु।।

Purankunri kaṇṭanaiyarenum akangkunri
Mookkir kariyaar uṭaittu.

## LIVING

He who lives life as it shoud be lived is united with God in heaven.

## LOVE

Love creates attraction towards others, this leads to friendship.

## LUST

Not looking at another's wife with a lustful eye is, for the wise, not only righteous conduct, but the very essence of their being.

## MASKS

There are many whose external appearance is pleasing like the red *kunri* seed, but whose hearts are black like its black edge.

## MODESTY

पिऱर्पऴियुं तंपऴियुं नाणुवार् नाणुक्कु
उऱैपति एन्नुं उलकु।।

Pirarpazhiyum tampazhiyum naaṇuvaar naaṇukku
Uraipati ennum ulaku.

नाणाल् उयिरै तुऱप्पर् उयिर्प्पोरुट्टाल्
नाण्तुऱवार् नाण् आळ्पवर्।।

Naaṇaal uyirai turappar uyirpporuṭṭaal
Naaṇturavār naaṇ aaḷpavar.

नाण् अकत्तिल्लार् इयक्कं मरप्पावै
नाणाल् उयिर् मरुट्टियट्रु।।

Naaṇ akattillaar iyakkam marappaavai
Naaṇaal uyir maruṭṭiyaṭṭru.

## NATURAL LAW

ऊऴिऱ् पेरुवलि यावुळ मट्रोन्ऱु
चूऴिनुं तान् मुन्तुऱुं।।

Oozhir peruvali yāvuḷa maṭṭronru
Choozhinum taan munturum.

## NOBILITY

अटुक्किय कोटि पेरिनुं कुटिप्पिऱन्तार्
कुन्ऱुव चेय्तल् इलर्।।

Aṭukkiya koṭi perinum kuṭippirantaar
Kunruva cheytal ilar.

## MODESTY

The world deems those as embodiments of modesty who conduct themselves in such a way as to prevent disgrace not only for themselves but others as well.

Great ones would give up life rather than their modesty.

Those without modesty (the shameless ones) are like puppets moved about by strings.

## NATURAL LAW

Even if we try to substitute natural law by something else, natural law prevails. Hence what can be stronger than it?

## NOBILITY

People of noble lineage never stoop to do wrong things, even if lured by millions in lucre.

कुटिपिऱन्तार् कण्विळङ्कुं कुट्ऱ्ं विचुम्पिन्
मतिक्कण् मऱुपोल् उयर्न्तु।।

Kuṭipirantaar kaṇviḷankum kuṭṭram vichumpin
Matikkaṇ marupol uyarntu.

अन्पु नाण् ओप्पुऱवु कण्णोट्टं वाय्मैयोटु
ऐन्तु चाल्पु ऊन्ऱिय तूण्।।

Anpu naaṇ oppuravu kaṇṇoṭṭam vaaymaiyoṭu
Aintu chaalpu oonriya tooṇ.

कोल्ला नलत्ततु नोन्मै पिऱर्तीमै
चोल्ला नलत्ततु चाल्पु।।

Kollaa nalattatu nonmai piṛarteemai
Chollaa nalattatu chaalpu.

इन्नाचेय्तार्क्कुं इनियवे चेय्याक्काल्
एन्न पयत्ततो चाल्पु।।

Innaacheytaarkkum iniyave cheyyaakkaal
Enna payattato chaalpu.

ऊऴि पेयरिनुं तांपेयरार् चान्ऱान्मैक्कु
आऴि येनप्पटुवार्।।

Oozhi peyarinum taampeyaraar chaanraanmaikku
Aazhi yenappaṭuvaar.

पण्पुटैयार्प्पट्टुण्डुलकं अतु इन्ऱेल्
मण्पुक्कु माय्वतु मन्।।

Paṇpuṭaiyaarppaṭṭuṇḍulakam atu inrel
Maṇpukku maayvatu man.

The fault of one born in a noble family will be patent to all, like the stain on the moon.

Love, modesty, helpfulness, compassion, truthfulness—these are the five pillars of nobility.

Penance is that self-discipline which is determined not to kill anyone,
Nobility is that good quality which refuses to slander others.

What is the use of nobility, if evil done is not repaid with goodness?

The noble ones remain as steadfast as the sea, even in times of deluge.

The world survives because of its good and noble ones, but for them it will go to ruin.

## OVERSHOOT

नुनिक्कोम्पर् एऱिनाऱ् अतु इऱन्तु ऊक्किन्
उयिर्क्किऱुति आकि विटुं।।

Nunikkompar erinaar atu irantu ookkin
Uyirkkiruti aaki viṭum.

## PAIN

उट्रनोय् नोन्ऱल् उयिर्क्कुरुकण् चेय्यामै
अट्रे तवत्तिर्कु उरु।।

Uṭṭranoy nonraal uyirkkurukaṇ cheyyaamai
Aṭṭre tavattirku uru.

## PLACE

कालाऴ्कळरिन् नरि अटुंकण् अञ्चा
वेलाळ् मुकत्त कळिऱु।।

Kaalaazhkaḷarin nari aṭumkaṇ añchaa
Velaaḷ mukatta kaḷiru.

## POOR, POVERTY

नऱ्पोरुळ् नन्कुणर्न्तु चोल्लिनुं नल्कूर्न्तार्
चोऱ्पोरुळ् चोर्वुपटुं।।

Narporuḷ nankuṇarntu chollinum nalkoorntār
Chorporuḷ chorvupaṭum.

अरंचारा नल्कुरवु ईन्ऱतायानुं
पिऱन्पोल नोक्कपटुं।।

Aramchaaraa nalkuravu eenratāyaanum
Piṛanpola nokkapaṭum.

## OVERSHOOT

Aiming beyond one's capacity, like trying to climb farther than the topmost branch of a tree, brings one to ruin.

## PAIN

The essence of self-discipline (or penance) is to bear any pain oneself, but not to cause any to others.

## PLACE

An elephant which can destroy spearheaded warriors, if caught in a mire, can be killed even by a jackal.

## POOR, POVERTY

Words of learning and wisdom spoken by the poor fall on deaf ears.

Even a mother will treat as outcast one who swerves from the path of rectitude, due to poverty.

## PROSPERITY

आक्कं अतर्विनाय्च्चेल्लुं अचैविला
ऊक्कं उडैयानुऴै।।

Aakkam atarvinaaycchellum achaivilaa
Ookkam uḍaiyaanuzhai.

## PUNISHMENT

ईन्नाचेय्तारै ओऱुत्तल् अवर् नाण
नन्नयञ्चेय्तु विटिल्।।

Īnnaacheytaarai oruttal avar naaṇa
Nannayañcheytu viṭil.

कोलैयिऱ् कोटियाऱै वेन्तोऱुत्तल्
पैङ्कूऴ् कळैकट्टतनोटु नेऱ्।।

Kolaiyir koṭiyaarai ventoruttal
Painkoozh kaḷaikaṭṭatanoṭu ner.

## REPUTATION

तोन्ऱिऱ् पुकऴोटु तोन्ऱुक अतिलाऱ्
तोन्ऱलिऱ् तोन्ऱामै नन्ऱु।।

Tonrir pukazhoṭu tonruka atilaar
Tonralir tonraamai nanru.

## RIGHTEOUSNESS

मनत्तुक्कण् माचिलन् आतल् अनैत्तऱन्
आकुल नीर पिऱ।।

Manattukkaṇ maachilan aatal anaittaran
Aakula neera pira.

## PROSPERITY

Prosperity will find its way to the person of undaunted will.

## PUNISHMENT

The best way to punish those who do harm is to make them feel ashamed by doing good to them.

Punishing those who commit heinous crimes like murder is like plucking out weeds in the interest of crops.

## REPUTATION

In any field, one should achieve good reputation,
Otherwise, it is better not to make a debut.

## RIGHTEOUSNESS

Being pure in mind is righteousness,
everything else is ostentation.

अऴुक्कारवावेकुऴि इन्नाच्चोल् नान्कुं
इऴुक्का इयन्रतरम्।।

Azhukkaaravāvekuḷi innaacchol naankum
Izhukkaa iyanrataram.

अन्पुं अरनुं उटैत्तायिन् इल्वाऴ्क्कै
पण्पुं पयनुं अतु।।

Anpum aranum uṭaittaayin ilvaazhkkai
Paṇpum payanum atu.

तक्कार् तकविलर् एन्पतवरवर्
एच्चत्तार् काण पटुम्।।

Takkaar takavilar enpatavaravar
Ecchattaar kaaṇa paṭum.

## RULER

इयट्रलुं ईट्टलुं कात्तलुं कात्त
वकुत्तलुं वल्लतरशु।।

Iyaṭṭralum eeṭṭalum kaattalum kaatta
Vakuttalum vallataraśu.

अल्लर्पट्टु आट्रातु अऴुतकण्णीर् अन्रे
चेल्वत्तै त्तेय्क्कुं पटै।।

Allarpaṭṭu aaṭṭraatu azhutakaṇṇeer anre
Chelvattai tteykkum paṭai.

अकलातु अणुकातु तीक्कायवार् पोल्क
इकल् वेन्तर् च्चेन्तोऴुकुवार्।।

Akalaatu aṇukaatu teekkaayvaar polka
Ikal ventar ccherntozhukuvaar.

Righteous deeds are those done without the four evils: Envy, greed, anger and harsh speech.

A loving heart and righteous deeds make this life virtuous and fruitful.

Whether a person was righteous or not will be known by what they leave behind (progeny, legacy, reputation etc.).

**RULER**

He is the wise ruler, who, while dispensing justice, generates revenues, enhances them and spends on a planned basis.

The tears shed by people, unable to suffer oppression, will become the weapon that destroys the power of the ruler.

Those who serve powerful rulers should neither be too near, nor too far, like the ones warming by the fireside.

## SIN

ईन्ऱाळ् पशिकाण्पान् आयिनुं चेय्यर्क
चान्ऱोर् पळिक्कुं विनै।।

Eenraaḷ paśikaaṇpaan aayinum cheyyarka
Chaanror pazhikkum vinai.

## SON

तन्तै मकर्काट्रुम् नन्ऱि अवैयत्तु
मुन्ति इरुप्पच्चेयल्।।

Tantai makarkaaṭrum nanri avaiyattu
Munti iruppaccheyal.

ईन्ऱ पोळुतिन् पेरितुवक्कुं तन्मकनै
च्चान्ऱोन् एन केट्ट ताय्।।

Eenra pozhutin perituvakkum tanmakanai
Cchaanron ena keṭṭa taay.

मकन् तन्तैक्काट्टुं उतवि इवन् तन्तै
एन्नोट्रान् कोल् एनुं चोल्।।

Makan tantaikkaaṭṭrum utavi ivan tantai
Ennoṭṭraan kol enum chol.

## TIME

ज्ञालङ्करुतिनुं कैकूटुं कालं
करुति इटत्तार् चेयिन्।।

Jñaalangkarutinum kaikooṭum kaalam
Karuti iṭattaar cheyin.

## SIN

Even if one's mother is starving, one should not do any sinful deed, which will be condemned by great ones.

## SON

The good that a parent needs to do to his son is to make him foremost in an assembly of scholars.

When a mother hears others speak highly of the greatness of her son, her joy exceeds the joy experienced by her when she gave birth to him.

When the public say: "what penance did the father perform to get such a (noble and learned) son" that is the return a son gives to his father.

## TIME

One can conquer even the whole world, if the right time and right place are selected.

## TONGUE

याकावारायिनुं नाकाक्क कावाक्काऱ्
चोकाप्पऱ् चोल्लिऴुक्कु पट्टु।।

Yaakaavaaraayinum naakaakka kaavaakkaar
Chokaappar chollizhukku paṭṭu.

## VEGETARIANISM

कोल्लान् पुलालै मऱुत्तानैक्कैकूप्पि
एल्ला उयिऱुं तोऴुम्।।

Kollaan pulaalai maruttaanaikkaikooppi
Ellaa uyirum tozhum.

## WATER

नीरिन्ऱमैयातुलकेतिन् याऱ्याऱ्क्कुं
वानिन्ऱमैया तोऴुक्कु।।

Neerinramaiyaatulaketin yaaryaarkkum
Vaaninramaiyaa tozhukku.

## WEALTH

पोरुळल्लवरै पोरुळाकच्चेय्युम्
पोरुळल्लतु इल्लै पोरुळ्।।

Poruḷallavarai poruḷaakaccheyyum
Poruḷallatu illai poruḷ.

## TONGUE

Whatever else one controls or not, one should control one's tongue, otherwise wrong words will bring ruin.

## VEGETARIANISM

Those who neither eat meat nor kill for meat are venerated by all living beings.

## WATER

Without water, the world cannot survive,
Without rain, there can be no provision of water.

## WEALTH

There is nothing other than wealth which can make those unfit for respect respectable.

## WICKED ONES

तेवर् अनैयर् कयवर् अवरुंतां
मेवन चेय्तोऴ्ुकलान्।।

Tevar anaiyar kayavar avarumtaam
Mevana cheydozhukalaan.

एट्ट्रिक्कु उरियर् कयवर् ओन्रु उट्ट्रुक्काल्
विट्ट्रक्कु उरियर् विरैन्तु।।

Eṭṭrirkku uriyar kayavar onru uṭṭrukkaal
Viṭṭrarkku uriyar viraintu.

## WIFE

इल्लतेन् इल्लवळ् माण्पानाल् उळ्ळतेन्
इल्लवळ् माणाक्कटै।।

Illaten illavaḷ maaṇpānaal uḷḷaten
Illavaḷ maaṇaakkaṭai.

## WISDOM

एप्पोरुळ् यार्यार्वाय्क्केट्पिनुं
मेय्प्पोरुळ् काण्पतऱिवु।।

Epporuḷ yaaryaarvaaykkeṭpinum
Meypporuḷ kaaṇpatarivu.

## WISHING ILL

मऱन्तुं पिऱन्केटु चूऴर्क चूऴिऩ्
अऱन्चूऴुं चूऴ्न्तवन् केटु।।

Marantum piranketu choozharka choozhin
Aranchoozhum choozhntavan keṭu.

## WICKED ONES

Wicked ones dare to do what they please.
In a way they can be compared to the celestials (who have the power to do what they please).

What are the wicked ones fit for?
Only to sell themselves as agents to do heinous things, when opportunities arise.

## WIFE

If there is a virtuous wife at home, life is full,
If there is not, life will be void.

## WISDOM

Whatever others may say about anything, wisdom lies in finding out the truth oneself.

## WISHING ILL

Even forgetfully, one should not wish ill for others,
For, if one does so, the Deity of righteousness will plot his ruin.

**WORDS**

इनिय उळवाक इन्नात कूरल्
कनि इरुप्प कायुकवर्न्तट्रु।।

Iniya uḷavaaka innaata kooral
Kani iruppa kāykavarntaṭṭru.

चोल्लुक चोल्लिर्पयनुटैय चोल्लर्क
चोल्लिऱ् पयनिलाच्चोल्।।

Cholluka chollirpayanuṭaiya chollarka
Chollir payanilaacchol.

चोल्लुक चोल्लैप्पिरितोर्चोल् अच्चोल्लै
वेल्लुंचोल् इन्मैयरिन्तु।।

Cholluka chollaippiritorchol acchollai
Vellumchol inmaiyarintu.

## WORDS

Using harsh words, when there are sweet words, is like plucking raw fruits, when sweet ones are available.

Speak meaningful words.
Avoid meaningless prattle.

Speak words, you are sure, will not be contradicted by other words.

# PART FOUR

# WONDROUS WHISPERS OF WISDOM FROM SUKRANITI

# WONDROUS WHISPERS OF WISDOM FROM SUKRANITI

## ADORNMENT

न भूषयत्यलंकारो न राज्यं न च पौरुषम्
न विद्या न धनं तादृग्यादृक् सौजन्यभूषणम्।।

Na bhooshayatyalankaaro na raajyam na cha paurusham
Na vidyaa na dhanam taadrigyaadṛk saujanya-bhooshaṇam.

## ALONE

एकः स्वादु न भुञ्जीत एकोऽर्थान्न विचिन्तयेत्
एको न गच्छेदध्वानं नैकः सुप्तेषु जागृयात्।।

Ekaḥ svaadu na bhuñjeeta ekoarthaanna vichintayet
Eko na gacchedadhvaanam naikah supteshu jaagṛyaat.

## ARGUMENT

स्वजनैर्न विरुध्येत न स्पर्धेत बलीयसा
न कुर्यात् स्त्रीबालवृद्धमूर्खेषु च विवादनम्।।

Svajanairna virudhyeta na spardheta baleeyasaa
Na kuryaat streebaalavṛddhamoorkheshu cha vivaadanam.

## ARROGANCE

न विद्यया न शौर्येण धनेनाभिजनेन च
न बलेन प्रमत्तः स्याच्चातिमानी कदाचन।।

Na vidyayaa na śauryeṇa dhanenaabhijanena cha
Na balena pramattaḥ syaachchaatimaanee kadaachana.
kadaachana.

## ADORNMENT

Kingdom, courage, learning and wealth do not adorn a man as much as the adornment of compassion.

## ALONE

One should not enjoy good food alone,
nor ponder over plans of action alone,
one should not go on a journey alone,
nor should one wake up alone, when others are asleep.

## ARGUMENT

One should not quarrel with one's people,
nor compete with the mighty,
one should also not enter into an argument with women, youngsters, the elderly or the foolish.

## ARROGANCE

One should not be arrogant with learning, courage, wealth, family or strength. One should never be excessively arrogant.

## ASSOCIATION

हस्त्यश्ववृषबालस्त्रीशुकानां शिक्षको यथा
तथा भवन्ति ते नित्यं संसर्गगुणधारकाः।।

Hastyaśvavṛshabaalastreeśukaanaam śikshako yathaa
Tathaa bhavanti te nityam samsargaguṇadhaarakaaḥ.

## ATTRACTION

विना दानार्जवभ्यां च भुव्यस्ति न वशीकरम्
दानक्षीणो विवधिष्णु शशी वक्रोऽप्यतः शुभः।।

Vinaa daanaarjavabhyaam cha bhuvyasti na vaśeekaram
Daanaksheeṇo vivadhishṇu śaśee vakropyataḥ śubhaḥ.

## BAD HABITS

षड्दोषाः पुरुषेणेह हातव्या भूतिमिच्छता
निद्रा तन्द्रा भयं क्रोध आलस्यं दीर्घसूत्रता
प्रभवन्ति विघाताय कार्यस्यैते न संशयः।।

Shaḍdoshaaḥ purusheṇeha haatavyaa bhootimicchataa
Nidraa tandraa bhayam krodha aalasyam deerghasootrataa
Prabhavanti vighaataaya kaaryasyaite na samśayaḥ.

## BELIEF

न प्रियाकथितं सम्यङ्मन्येतानुभवं विना
अपराधं मातृस्नुषा भ्रातृपत्नीसपत्निजम्।।

Na priyaakathitam samyangmanyetaanubhavam vinaa
Aparaadham maatrisnushaa bhraatripatneesapatnijam.

## ASSOCIATION

The elephant, horse, bull, young boy, woman and the parrot become good or bad due to association, depending on the teacher.

## ATTRACTION

There is nothing in the world more attractive than giving and being gentle,
The crescent moon, exhausted by giving nectarlike light, and yet hopeful of replenishment, looks attractive in its gentility.

## BAD HABITS

In this world, a person who desires to attain prosperity has to give up six bad habits:
Excessive sleep, inertia, fear, anger, laziness, and procrastination, for these can destroy achievement of tasks. There is no doubt about this.

## BELIEF

One should not accept what the beloved says about an error committed by mother, daughter-in-law, sister-in-law or cowife without personal experience or examination.

## CAPTIVATION

नहीदृशं संवननं त्रिषु लोकेषु विद्यते
दया मैत्री च भूतेषु दानं च मधुरा च वाक्।।

Naheedṛśam samvananam trishu lokeshu vidyate
Dayaa maitree cha bhooteshu daanam cha madhuraa cha vaak.

सद्भावेन हरेन्मित्रं सद्भावेन च बान्धवान्
स्त्रीभृत्यौ प्रेममानाभ्यां दाक्षिणेनेतरं जनम्।।

Sadbhaavena harenmitram sadbhaavena cha bāndhavaan
Streebhrityau premamaanaabhyaam daakshiṇenetaram janam.

भार्या पुत्रोप्युद्विजते कटुवाक्या दुग्रदण्डतः
पशवोऽपि वशं यान्ति दानैश्च मृदुभाषणैः।।

Bhaaryaa putropyudvijate kaṭuvaakyaa dugradaṇḍataḥ
Paśavopi vaśam yaanti daanaiścha mṛdubhaashaṇaiḥ.

## CASTE

न जात्या ब्राह्मणश्चात्र क्षत्रियो वैश्य एव न
न शूद्रो न च वै म्लेच्छो भेदिता गुणकर्मभिः।।

Na jaatyaa brāhmaṇaśchaatra kshatriyo vaiśya eva na
Na śoodro na cha vai mleccho bheditaa guṇakarmabhiḥ.

## COMPASSION

आनृशंस्यं परो धर्मः सर्वप्राणभृतां यत्
तस्माद्राजाऽऽनृशंस्येन पालयेत्कृपणं जनम्।।

Aanriśamsyam paro dharmaḥ sarvapraaṇabhṛtaam yat
Tasmaadraajaanṛśamsyena paalayetkṛpaṇam janam.

## CAPTIVATION

There is no captivation mantra in the three worlds greater than these:
Compassion towards all beings, friendship, donation and sweet speech.

Friends and relations should be captivated by good attitude, wife and servants by love and respect, and all others by compassion.

With harsh words and severe punishment, even one's wife and son revolt.
With sweet speech and gifts even animals can be won over.

## CASTE

Here (in this world), by caste no one is Brahmin, Kshatriya, Vaisya, Sudra or an outcaste, they are differentiated only by their qualities and actions.

## COMPASSION

Compassion is considered the supreme duty of all beings, Hence the ruler should protect with compassion poor, helpless people.

## CRIME

अग्निदो गरदश्चैव शस्त्रोन्मत्तो धनापहः
क्षेत्रदारहरश्चैतान् षड् विद्यादाततायिनः।।

Agnido garadaśchaiva śastronmatto dhanaapahaḥ
Kshetradaaraharaśchaitaan shaḍ vidyaadaatataayinaḥ.

## DEATH

स्त्रीभिर्जितो ऋणी नित्यं सुदरिद्रश्च याचकः
गुणहीनोऽर्थहीनः सन् मृता एते सजीविकाः।।

Streebhirjito ṛṇee nityam sudaridraścha yaachakaḥ
Guṇaheenoarthaheenaḥ san mṛtaa ete sajeevikaaḥ.

## DESTRUCTION

कुमन्त्रिभिर्नृपो रोगी कुवैद्यैः कुनृपैः प्रजा
कुसन्तत्या कुलं चात्मा कुबुद्धया हीयतेऽनिशम्।।

Kumantribhirnṛpo rogee kuvaidyaiḥ kunṛpaiḥ prajaa
Kusantatyaa kulam chaatmaa kubuddhyaa heeyate aniśam.

## DEVICE

अयोऽभेद्यमुपायेन द्रवतामुपनीयते
लोक प्रसिद्धमेवैतद् वारिवह्नोर्नियामकम्
उपायोपगृहीतेन तेनैतत् परिशोष्यते
उपायेन पदं मूर्ध्नि न्यस्यते मत्तहस्तिनाम्।।

Ayoabhedyamupaayena dravataamupaneeyate
Loka prasiddhamevaitad vaarivahnorniyaamakam
Upaayopagṛheetena tenaitat pariśoshyate
Upaayena padam moordhni nyasyate mattahastinaam.

## CRIME

One who sets fire, one who administers poison, one who is obsessed with using weapons, one who steals other's wealth, one who takes away another's land and one who steals another's wife, these six are the ones who commit the most heinous crimes.

## DEATH

He who is under the spell of women, is ever indebted, is very poor, ever begs others, is without any good quality or has no money, is to be deemed dead, though living.

## DESTRUCTION

The ruler is destroyed by bad counsellors,
the patient by inept physicians,
the people by bad rulers,
the family by bad progeny,
and self by bad intellect.

## DEVICE

Even the hardest metal can be liquefied by proper device,
It is well known that water puts out fire,
but by using a proper device fire can dry up water,
with proper device, one can set foot even on the forehead of a wild elephant.

## DISCORD

न भेदं जनयेयुर्वै नृनार्योः स्वामिभृत्ययोः
भ्रातृणां गुरुशिष्याणां न कुर्युः पितृपुत्रयोः।।

Na bhedam janayeyurvai nṛnaaryoḥ swaamibhṛtyayoḥ
Bhraatṛṇaam guruśishyaaṇaam na kuryuḥ pitṛputrayoḥ.

## DISREGARD

सर्पोऽग्निर्दुर्जनो राजा जामाता भगिनीसुतः
रोगः शत्रुर्नावमान्योऽप्यल्प इत्युपचारितः।।

Sarpoagnirdurjano raajaa jāmaataa bhagineesutaḥ
Rogaḥ śatrurnaavamaanyoapyalpa ityupacharitaḥ.

## DISREPUTE

श्रीमत्तः पुरुषो वेत्ति न दुष्कीर्तिमजो यथा
स्वमूत्रगन्धं मूत्रेण मुखमासिञ्चते स्वकम्।।

Śreemattaḥ purusho vetti na dushkeertimajo yathaa
Svamootragandham mootreṇa mukhamaasiñchate svakam.

## DISRESPECT

मातृणां पितृणां चैव पूज्यानां विदुषामपि
नावमानं नोपहासं कुर्युः सद्वृत्तशालिनाम्।।

Maatṛṇaam pitṛṇaam chaiva poojyaanaam vidushaamapi
Naavamaanam nopahaasam kuryuḥ sadvrittaśaalinaam.

## DISCORD

One should not cause discord between husband and wife, between servant and master, between brothers, between teacher and disciple, and between father and son.

## DISREGARD

The serpent, fire, wicked people, the ruler, the son-in-law, nephew (sister's son), disease, and enemy—these should never be ignored or disregarded (effort should always be made to keep them in check).

## DISREPUTE

The person, who is dizzy with his wealth, does not realise his ill repute, like the goat which keeps soaking its face, already stinking with urine, in urine.

## DISRESPECT

One should not mock at or ridicule or disrespect:
Mother, father, venerable ones, learned scholars and those who do good deeds.

## DOS & DON'TS

काले हितमिताहारविहारी विधसाशनः
अदीनात्मा च सुस्वप्नः शुचिः स्यात्सर्वदा नरः।।

Kaale hitamitaahaaravihāree vidhasāśanaḥ
Adeenātmaa cha susvapnaḥ śuchiḥ syaatsarvadaa naraḥ.

कुर्याद्विहारमाहारं निर्हारं विजने सदा
व्यवसायी सदा च स्यात्सुखं व्यायाममभ्यसेत्।।

Kuryaadvihaaramaahāram nirhaaram vijane sadaa
Vyavasaayee sadaa cha syātsukham vyaayaamamabhyaset.

काले हितं मितं ब्रूयादविसंवादि पेशलम्
पूर्वाभिभाषी सुमुखः सुशीलः करुणामृदुः
नैकः सुखी न सर्वत्र विश्रब्धो न च शङ्कितः।।

Kaale hitam mitam brooyādavisamvaadi peśalam
Poorvaabhibhaashee sumukhaḥ suśeelaḥ karuṇaamṛduḥ
Naikaḥ sukhee na sarvatra viśrabdho na cha śankitaḥ

नाकार्ये तु मतिं कुर्याद् द्राक्स्वकार्यं प्रसाधयेत्
उद्योगेन बलेनैव बुद्धया धैर्येण साहसात्
पराक्रमेणार्जवेन मानमुत्सृज्य साधकः।।

Naakaarye tu matim kuryaad draaksvakāryam prasaadhayet
Udyogena balenaiva buddhyaa dhairyeṇa sāhasaat
Paraakrameṇaarjavena maanamutsṛjya saadhakaḥ.

मातृपितृगुरुस्वामिभ्रातृपुत्रसखिष्वपि
न विरुध्येन्नापकुर्यान्मनसाऽपि क्षणं क्वचित्।।

Maatṛpitṛguruswaamibhraatṛputrasakhishvapi
Na virudhyennaapakuryaanmanasaapi kshaṇam kvachit.

## DOS & DON'TS

Man should always eat in time limited quantities of food, and then relax, eat remnants of ritual offerings, never show self-pity, sleep well and remain pure (in mind, word and deed).

One should indulge in sex, dine and excrete in private, should be industrious always and practise light physical exercise.

One should speak sweetly, timely, briefly, tenderly, without arrogance,
One should ever be pleasant-faced, happy, well-behaved and compassionate,
One should not enjoy pleasures alone (but share them with others).
One should not trust everyone nor doubt everyone.

Never think of doing bad things,
One should accomplish tasks by concerted effort, strength, intelligence, courage, daring, heroism, simplicity, giving up arrogance.

One should not, even for a moment, antagonise or act against mother, father, teacher, master, brother, son or friend.

मूकोऽन्धो बधिरः खञ्जः स्वापत्काले भवेन्नरः
अन्यथा दुःखमाप्नोति हीयते व्यवहारतः।।

Mookoandho badhiraḥ khñjaḥ svaapatkaale bhavennaraḥ
Anyathaa dukhamaapnoti heeyate vyavahaarataḥ.

**DUTY**

अरक्षितारं नृपतिं ब्राह्मणं चातपस्विनम्
धनिकं चाप्रदातारं देवा घ्नन्ति त्यजन्त्यधः।।

Arakshitaaram nṛpatim brāhmaṇam chaatapasvinam
Dhanikam chaapradaataaram devaa ghnanti tyajantyadhaḥ.

**EFFORT**

उद्योगेनैव सिध्यन्ति कार्याणि न मनोरथैः
न हि सुप्तमृगेन्द्रस्य निपतन्ति गजाः मुखे।।

Udyogenaiva sidhyanti kaaryaaṇi na manorathaiḥ
Na hi suptamṛgendrasya nipatanti gajaaḥ mukhe.

**ENEMY**

सामैव प्रथमं श्रेष्टं दानं तु तदनन्तरम्
सर्वदा भेदनं शत्रोर्दण्डनं प्राणसंशये।।

Saamaiva prathamam śreshṭam daanam tu tadanantaram
Sarvadaa bhedanam śatrordaṇḍanam praaṇasamśaye.

**EVIL ONE**

अन्योदयासहिष्णुश्च छिद्रदर्शी विनिन्दकः
द्रोहशीलः स्वान्तमलः प्रसन्नास्यः खलः स्मृतः।।

Anyodayaasahishṇuścha cchidradarśee vinindakaḥ
Drohaśeelaḥ svaantamalaḥ prasannaasyaḥ khalaḥ smṛtaḥ.

In difficult times, a man should behave like
a dumb person (in speaking ill of others),
a blind one (in seeing others' faults),
a deaf one (in listening to slander about others),
and a lame person (in rushing to express indignation).
Otherwise, he will meet with sorrow and things go awry.

## DUTY

A ruler who does not protect (his people),
a Brahmin who is not self-disciplined,
a rich person who does not donate his wealth,
all these are either destroyed or pushed down by the gods.

## EFFORT

Only through effort can things be achieved, not by mere dreams.
Elephants do not fall automatically into a sleeping lion's mouth.

## ENEMY

With an enemy, first a peaceful approach is preferable,
if it fails, gifts should be tried,
if that also fails, division tactic should be tried.
Punishment should be resorted to as the last resort, when life is in danger.

## EVIL ONE

He is considered the evil one, who:
cannot tolerate another's prosperity,
always finds fault,
derides others,
harbours hatred,
and is pleasant-faced, even though the mind is soiled.

## EXCESS

अत्यटन चानशनमतिमैथुनमैव च
अत्यायासश्च सर्वेषां द्रागजराकरणं महत्
अत्यायासो हि विद्यासु जराकारी कलासु च।।

Atyaṭana chaanaśanamatimaithunamaiva cha
Atyaayaasaścha sarveshaam draagjaraakaraṇam mahat
Atyaayaaso hi vidyaasu jaraakaari kalaasu cha.

नातिक्रौर्यं नातिशाठ्यं धारयेन्नतिमार्दवम्
नातिवादं नातिकार्यासक्तिमत्याग्रहं न च।।

Naatikrauryam naatiśaaṭhyam dhārayennatimaardavam
Naativaadam naatikaaryaasaktimatyaagraham na cha.

## FAMILY

कुटुम्बभरणार्थेषु यत्नवान्न भवेच्च यः
तस्य सर्वगुणैः किन्तु जीवन्नेव मृतश्च सः।।

Kuṭumbabharaṇaartheshu yatnavaanna bhavechcha yaḥ
Tasya sarvaguṇaiḥ kintu jeevanneva mṛtaścha saḥ.

## FELONY

आततायित्वमापन्नो ब्राह्मणः शूद्रवत् स्मृतः
नाततायिवधे दोषो हन्तुर्भवति कश्चन।।

Aatataayitvamaapanno brāhmaṇaḥ śoodravat smṛtaḥ
Naatataayivadhe dosho hanturbhavati kaśchana.

## EXCESS

Excessive travelling, excessive fasting, excessive sex, excessive work and toil, all these bring on aging very fast. Putting in too much effort to learn all the arts and sciences also causes premature aging.

One should not have excessive anger, excessive obstinacy, excessive softness, excessive arguments, excessive attachment to things and excessive greed.

## FAMILY

A person who does not put in effort to look after his family, even though equipped with all good qualities, is to be deemed dead, even though living.

## FELONY

A brahmin who commits felony is deemed a Sudra,
there is no sin attached in killing one who commits felony.

## FOOD

अन्नं न निन्द्यात्सुस्वस्थः स्वीकुर्यात्प्रीतिभोजनम्
आहारं प्रवरं विद्यात् षड्रसं मधुरोत्तरम्।।

Annam na nindyaatsusvasthaḥ sveekuryaatpreetibhojanam
Aahaaram pravaram vidyaat shaḍrasam madhurottaram.

## FOOL

एकस्मिन्नधिकारे तु यो द्वाधिकरोति सः
मूर्खो जीवद् द्विभार्यश्च ह्यतिविस्त्रम्भवांस्तथा
महाधनाशो ह्यलसः स्त्रीभिर्निर्जित एव हि
तथा यः साक्षितां पृच्छेच्चोरजाराततायिषु।।

Ekasminnavadhikaare tu yo dvaadhikaroti saḥ
Moorkho jeevad dvibhaaryaścha hyativistrambhavaamstathaa
Mahaadhanaaśo hyalasaḥ streebhirnirjita eva hi
Tathaa yaḥ saakshitaam pṛcchechchorajaaraatataayishu.

यो जानात्यर्जितुं सम्यगर्जितं न हि रक्षितुम्
नातः परतरो मूर्खो वृथा तस्यार्जनश्रमः।।

Yo jaanaatyarjitum samyagarjitam na hi rakshitum
Naataḥ parataro moorkho vṛthaa tasyaarjanaśramaḥ.

## FORT

एकः शतं योधयति दुर्गस्थोऽस्त्रधरो यदि
शतं दशसहस्राणि तस्माद् दुर्गं समाश्रयेत्।।

Ekah śatam yodhayati durgasthoastradharo yadi
Śatam daśasahasraaṇi tasmaad durgam samaaśrayet.

## FOOD

Food should never be despised, when in good health, one should accet food offred with satissfaction.
That food should be deemed superior which has all the six variant tastes (sour, salty, bitter, sweet, hot and lemony), with sweetness topping it all.

## FOOL

He is a fool:
Who appoints two persons to discharge one responsibility,
Who, while one's wife is alive, marries a second and trusts them both implicitly,
Who is desirous of acquiring great wealth and yet remains lazy,
Who is under the control of women, and
Who asks for witness's evidence in matters of theft, spying and other heinous crimes.

There is no greater fool than the one who knows well how to earn but cannot save what is earned, because his effort to earn wealth has gone in vain.

## FORT

One armed soldier on the fort can fight a hundred coming from outside, a hundred soldiers on the fort can fight ten thousand from outside. Hence access to the fort is desirable.

## FOUR GOALS & STAGES OF LIFE

विद्यार्थं ब्रह्मचारी स्यात् सर्वेषां पालने गृही
वानप्रस्थ: सन्दमने सन्यासी मोक्षसाधने।।

Vidyaartham brahmachaaree syaat sarveshaam paalane gṛhee
Vaanaprasthaḥ sandamane sanyaasee mokshasaadhane.

## FRIENDSHIP

य: साहाय्यं सदा कुर्यात्प्रतीपन्न वदेत्क्वचित्
सत्यं हितं वक्ति याति दत्ते गृह्णाति मित्रताम्।।

Yaḥ saahaayyam sadaa kuryātprateepanna vadetkvachit
Satyam hitam vakti yaati datte grihṇaati mitrataam.

यस्येच्छेदुत्तमां मैत्रीं कुर्यान्नार्थाभिलाषकम्
परोक्षे तद्रहश्चारं तत्स्त्रीसम्भाषणं तथा
तन्न्यूनदर्शनं नैव तत्प्रतीपविवादनम्
असाहाय्यं च तत्कार्ये ह्यनिष्टोपेक्षणं न च।।

Yasyeccheduttamaam maitreem kuryaannaarthaabhilāshakam
Parokshe tadrahaśchaaram tatstreesambhaashaṇam tathaa
Tannyoonadarśanam naiva tatprateepavivaadanam
Asaahaayyam cha tatkaarye hyanishṭopekshaṇam na cha.

## FRUITS

विद्यायाश्च फलं ज्ञानं विनयश्च फलं श्रिय:
यज्ञदाने बलफलं सद्रक्षणमुदाहृतम्।।

Vidyaayaaścha phalam jñaanam vinayaścha phalam śriyaḥ
Yajñadaane balaphalam sadrakshaṇamudāhṛtam.

## FOUR GOALS & STAGES OF LIFE

To acquire learning, one should be a celibate,
to protect everyone, one should be a householder,
the vaanaprastha state (going to the forest) is to control the senses,
and the final stage of being a *sanyasi* or recluse is to attain liberation.

## FRIENDSHIP

He who ever helps, never speaks against, speaks truth sweetly, and gives financial assistance in time becomes a friend.

If one desires intimate friendship with someone,
one should not covet his wealth,
one should not enter his inner apartments or speak to his wife in secret,
one should not notice his defects,
nor should one speak against him,
one should help him and not desert him in difficulties.

## FRUITS

The fruit of learning is wisdom and humility,
the fruit of wealth is performance of rites and donations,
the fruit of strength is the protection of good ones.

## HAPPINESS

सुभार्या सुष्ठु चापत्यं सुविद्या सुधनं सुहृत्
सुदासदास्यौ सद्देहः सद्वेश्म सुनृपः सदा
गृहिणां हि सुखायालं दशैतानि न चान्यथा।।

Subhaaryaa sushṭhu chaapatyam suvidyaa sudhanam suhṛt
Sudaasadaasyau saddehaḥ sadveśma sunripaḥ sadaa
Gṛhiṇaam hi sukhaayaalam daśaitaani na chānyathaa.

सुखार्थाः सर्वभूतानां मताः सर्वाः प्रवृत्तयः
सुखं च न विना धर्मात्तस्माद्धर्म परो भवेत्।।

Sukhaarthaaḥ sarvabhootaanaam mataaḥ sarvaaḥ pravrittayaḥ
Sukham cha na vinaa dharmaattasmaaddharma paro bhavet.

मूर्खः पुत्रोऽधवा कन्या चण्डी भार्या दरिद्रता
नीचसेवा ऋणं नित्यं नैतत्षट्कं सुखाय च।।

Moorkhaḥ putroadhavaa kanyaa chaṇḍee bhaaryaa daridrataa
Neechasevaa ṛṇam nityam naitatshaṭkam sukhaaya cha.

पारतन्त्र्यात्परं दुःखं न स्वातन्त्र्यात्परं सुखम्
अप्रवासी गृही नित्यं स्वतन्त्रः सुखमेधते।।

Paaratantryaatparam dukham na svaatantryaatparam sukham
Apravaasee gṛhee nityam svatantraḥ sukhamedhate.

## HELL

अकीर्तिरेव नरको नान्योऽस्ति नरको दिवि
नरदेहाद्विना त्वन्यो देहो नरक एव सः।।

Akeertireva narako naanyoasti narako divi
Naradehaadvinaa tvanyo deho naraka eva saḥ.

## HAPPINESS

Ten things conduce to happiness for householders:
A good spouse, a good son, good learning, righteously earned wealth, good friend, good servant, good maid, a healthy body, good house and a good ruler.

The acts of all beings are directed towards attaining happiness.
But there will be no happiness without righteousness. Hence everyone should adhere to righteousness.

These six do not contribute to happiness:
Idiotic son, widowed daughter, quarrelsome spouse, poverty, service under bad masters, and constant indebtedness.

There is no greater sorrow than being under someone else's control, there is no greater happiness than freedom,
He who does not go abroad, but lives independently in his own house attains happiness.

## HELL

Disrepute is the only hell, there is no other hell in the other world.
Being embodied as anything other than a human being is hell as well.

## HELP

सदाऽल्पमप्युकृतं महत् साधुषु जायते
मन्यते सर्षपादल्पं महच्चोपकृतं खलः।।

Sadaalpamapyukṛtam mahat saadhushu jaayate
Manyate sarshapaadalpam mahachchopakritam khalaḥ.

## HERO

भर्तुरर्थे च यः शूरो विक्रमेद्वाहिनीमुखे
भयान्न विनिवर्तेत तस्य स्वर्गोह्यनन्तकः।।

Bharturarthe cha yaḥ śooro vikramedvaahinee mukhe
Bhayaanna vinivarteta tasya svargohyanantakaḥ.

न हि शौर्यात्परं किञ्चित्त्रिषु लोकेषु विद्यते
शूरः सर्वं पालयति शूरे सर्वं प्रतिष्ठितम्।।

Na hi śauryaatparam kiñchittrishu lokeshu vidyate
Śooraḥ sarvam paalayati śoore sarvam pratishṭhitam.

## HUSBAND

नास्ति भर्तृसमो नाथो नास्ति भर्तृसमं सुखम्
विसृज्य धनसर्वस्वं भर्ता वै शरणं स्त्रियः।।

Naasti bhartrisamo naatho naasti bhartrisamam sukham
Visrijya dhanasarvasvam bhartaa vai śaraṇam striyaḥ.

## HELP

Good persons consider even a small help rendered as big, whereas evil ones treat even a great help as trifling as a mustard seed.

## HERO

The valorous hero who, for the sake of his master, fights at the forefront of the army and does not retreat out of fear, his is eternal heaven.

There is nothing greater in the three worlds than heroic valour.
The courageous hero protects everything, on him depends everything.

## HUSBAND

For a woman, her husband (who husbands her well) is unequalled as a protector.
No one else can give such pleasure as a husband.
Hence women should seek refuge in the husband, giving up everything else.
The husband is a woman's wealth and everything of value.

## INTERESTS

नाध्यापने नाध्ययने न देवे न गुरौ द्विजे
न कलासु न सङ्गीते सेवायां नार्जवे स्त्रियाम्
न शौर्ये न च तपसि साहित्ये रमते मनः
यस्य मुक्तः खलः किं वा नररूपपशुश्च सः।।

Naadhyaapane naadhyayane na deve na gurau dvije
Na kalaasu na sangeete sevaayaam naarjave striyaam
Na śaurye na cha tapasi saahitye ramate manaḥ
Yasya muktaḥ khalaḥ kim vaa nararoopapaśuścha saḥ.

## KILLING

उद्यम्य शस्त्रमायान्तं भ्रूणमप्याततायिनम्
निहत्य भ्रूणहा न स्यादहत्वा भ्रूणहा भवेत्।।

Udyamya śastramaayaantam bhrooṇamapyaatataayinam
Nihatya bhrooṇahā na syaadahatvaa bhrooṇahaa bhavet.

## LAZINESS

यतते नैव कालेऽपि क्रियां कर्तुं च सालसः
न सिद्धिस्तस्य कुत्रापि स नश्यति च सान्वयः।।

Yatate naiva kaaleapi kriyaam kartum cha saalasaḥ
Na siddhistasya kutraapi sa naśyati cha saanvayaḥ.

## LENDING

पराधीनं नैव कुर्यात्तरुणीं धन पुस्तकम्
कृतं चेल्लभते दैवाद् भ्रष्टां नष्टं विमर्दितम्।।

Paraadheenam naiva kuryaattaruṇeem dhana pustakam
Kṛtam chellabhate daivaad bhrashṭaam nashṭam vimarditam.

## INTERESTS

He whose mind is not interested in teaching or learning, in the service of God, teacher or learned preceptors, in fine arts or music, women, heroism, penance or literature, is either a liberated one or an evil one or an animal in the form of a man.

## KILLING

If even a young boy comes attacking with a weapon, he should be killed.
In such an event there is no sin of killing a young boy.

## LAZINESS

He who does not put in the effort in time to do a thing, is called the lazy one. Such a person does not achieve anything. He perishes with his family.

## LENDING

One should never leave under another's control one's young bride, wealth or books. Even if by good fortune these are got back, they will (respectively) be soiled, reduced in value and tattered.

## MASTER-SERVANT

भृत्यः स एव सुश्लोकोऽपि नापत्तौ स्वामिनं त्यजेत्
स्वामी स एव विज्ञेयो भृत्यार्थं जीवितं त्यजेत्।।

Bhrityaḥ sa eva suślokoapi naapattau swaaminam tyajet
Swaamee sa eva vijñeyo bhṛtyaartham jeevitam tyajet.

## MISFORTUNE

मातुः प्रियायाः पुत्रस्य धनस्य च विनाशनम्
बाल्ये मध्ये च वार्धक्ये महापापफलं क्रमात्।।

Maatuḥ priyaayaaḥ putrasya dhanasya cha vinaaśanam
Baalye madhye cha vaardhakye mahaapaapaphalam kramaat.

## MODESTY

आहारे व्यवहारे च त्यक्तलज्जः सुखी भवेत्।

Aahaare vyavahaare cha tyaktalajjaḥ sukhee bhavet.

## MONEY

धनं मैत्रीकरं दाने चादाने शत्रुकारकम्।

Dhanam maitreekaram daane chaadaane śatrukaarakam.

## POOR

दोषा अपि गुणायन्ते दोषायन्ते गुणा अपि
धनवतो निर्धनस्य निन्द्यते निर्धनोऽखिलैः।।

Doshaa api guṇaayante doshaayante guṇaa api
Danavato nirdhanasya nindyate nirdhano akhilaiḥ.

## MASTER-SERVANT

He is the valued servant who, in times of danger, gives up his life for the master.
He is the real master who gives up his life for the servant.

## MISFORTUNE

Losing one's mother in childhood, a dear wife in youth, and son and money in old age is the result of great sins committed in earlier births.

## MODESTY

He who gives up modesty while eating and doing business is happy.

## MONEY

At the time of giving, money creates friendship,
at the time of taking it back, money causes enmity.

## POOR

Even defects become good qualities in the wealthy.
Even good qualities become defects for the poor.
People despise one without wealth.

## PREFERENCE

परगृह निवासाद्ह्यरण्ये निवसनं वरम्
प्रदुष्टभार्यागार्हस्थ्याद्भैक्ष्यं वा मरणं वरम्।।

Paragṛhanivaasaadhyaraṇye nivasanam varam
Pradushṭabhāryāgārhasthyādbhaikshyam vā maraṇam varam.

## PROGRESS

आदौ वरं निर्धनत्वं धनिकत्वमनन्तरम्
तथादौ पादगमनं यानगत्वमनन्तरम्
सुखाय कल्पते नित्यं दुःखाय विपरीतकम्।।

Aadau varam nirdhanatvam dhanikatvamanantaram
Tathaadau paadagamanam yaanagatvamanantaram
Sukhaaya kalpate nityam dukhaaya vipareetakam.

## RESIDENCE

विरुद्धो यत्र नृपतिर्धनिकः श्रोत्रियो भिषक्
आचारश्च तथा देशो न तत्र दिवसं वसेत्।।

Viruddho yatra nṛpatirdhanikaḥ śrotriyo bhishak
Aachaaraścha tathaa deśo na tatra divasam vaset.

अविवेकी यत्र राजा सभ्या यत्र तु पाक्षिकाः
सन्मार्गोज्झितविद्वांसः साक्षिणोऽनृतवादिनः
दुरात्मनां च प्राबल्यं स्त्रीणां नीचजनस्य च
तत्र नेच्छेद्धनं मानं वसतिं चापि जीवितम्।।

Avivekee yatra raajaa sabhyaa yatra tu paakshikaaḥ
Sanmārgojjhitavidwaamsaḥ saakshiṇoanṛtavaadinaḥ
Duraatmanaam cha praabalyam streeṇaam neechajanasya cha
Tatra neccheddhanam maanam vasatim chaapi jeevitam.

## PREFERENCE

It is better to stay in the jungle than in somebody else's house, it is better to be a recluse or die than be a householder with an adulterous wife.

## PROGRESS

It is better to be poor first and rich later,
better to walk on foot first and ride in vehicles later,
This conduces to happiness, the reverse to sorrow.

## RESIDENCE

Where the ruler, the wealthy, the intellectuals, the doctors, customs and the country itself are against you, you should not stay even for a day.

Where the ruler is devoid of discretion,
the members of the royal assembly are partial and prejudiced,
the scholars have given up the righteous path,
the witnesses speak falsehood,
and evil and wicked people and women predominate,
one should not desire to live and hope for the protection of wealth, respect, residence and life.

## RESPECT

अधमा धनमिच्छन्ति धनमानौ मध्यमाः
उत्तमा मानमिच्छन्ति मानो हि महतां धनम्।।

Adhamaa dhanamicchanti dhanamaanau madhyamaaḥ
Uttamaa maanamicchanti maano hi mahataam dhanam.

## RESULTS

स्वामित्वं चैव दातृत्वं धनिकत्वं तपः फलम्
एनसः फलमर्थित्वं दास्यत्वं च दरिद्रता।।

Swāmitvam chaiva daatṛtvam dhanikatvam tapaḥ phalam
Enasaḥ phalamarthitvam daasyatvam cha daridrataa.

## RULER

शासनं त्वीदृशं कार्यं राज्ञा नित्यं प्रजासु च
दासे भृत्येऽथ भार्यायां पुत्रे शिष्येऽपि वा क्वचित्
वाग्दण्डपरुषं नैव कार्यं मद्देशसंस्थितैः।।

Śaasanam tveedṛśam kaaryam raajñaa nityam prajaasu cha
Daase bhṛtyeatha bhaaryaayaam putre śishyeapi vaa kvachit
Vaagdaṇḍaparusham naiva kaaryam maddeśasamsthitaiḥ.

दुष्टनिग्रहणं दानं प्रजायाः परिपालनम्
यजनं राजसूयादेः कोशानां न्यायतोऽर्जनम्
करदीकरणं राज्ञां रिपूणां परिमर्दनम्
भूमेरुपार्जनं भूयो राजवृत्तं तु चाष्टधा।।

Dushṭanigrahaṇam daanam prajaayaaḥ paripaalanam
Yajanam raajasooyaadeḥ kośaanaam nyaayatoarjanam
Karadeekaraṇam raajñaam ripooṇaam parimardanam
Bhoomerupaarjanam bhooyo raajavṛttam tu chaashṭadhaa.

## RESPECT

Low people desire wealth, medium type desire both wealth and respect, superior ones desire only respect, for respect is the wealth of the great.

## RESULTS

Being a ruler, being a donor, being rich—these are the results of penance,
Being a beggar, a servant and being poor—these are the results of sin.

## RULER

A ruler should ever issue instructions to his people that those residing in his domain should never speak harsh words or mete out harsh punishment to servants, spouse, children and students.

Eight are the duties of the ruler:
Punishing the wicked,
giving donations,
protecting the people,
performing sacrifices like the *Rajasooya*,
enhancing treasury resources in a legal, just way,
getting taxes from other (subordinate) rulers,
destroying the arrogance of enemies,
and always expanding the boundaries of his state.

न वर्धितं बलं यैस्तु न भूपाः करदीकृताः
न प्रजाः पालिताः सम्यक्ते वै षण्ढतिला नृपाः।।

Na vardhitam balam yaistu na bhoopaaḥ karadeekṛtaaḥ
Na prajaaḥ paalitaaḥ samyakte vai shaṇḍhatilaa nṛpaaḥ.

न कालवर्षी पर्जन्यस्तत्र भूर्न महाफला
जायते राष्ट्रह्रासश्च शत्रुवृद्धिर्धनक्षयः।।

Na kaalavarshee parjanyastatra bhoorna mahaaphalaa
Jaayate raashṭrahraasaścha śatruvṛddhirdhanakshayaḥ.

शौर्यं पाण्डित्यवक्तृत्वं दातृत्वं न त्यजेत्क्वचित्
बलं पराक्रमं नित्यमुत्थानं चापि भूमिपः।।

Śauryam paaṇḍityavaktṛtvam daatritvam na tyajetkvachit
Balam paraakramam nityamutthaanam chaapi bhoomipaḥ.

परस्त्रीसङ्गमे कामो लोभो नान्यधनेषु च
स्वप्रजादण्डने क्रोधो नैव धार्यो नृपैः कदा।।

Parastreesangame kaamo lobho naanyadhaneshu cha
Svaprajaadaṇḍane krodho naiva dhaaryo nṛpaiḥ kadaa.

न हि स्वसुखमन्विच्छन् पीडयेत्कृपणं जनम्
कृपणः पीड्यमानः स्वमृत्युना हन्ति पार्थिवम्।।

Na hi svasukhamanvicchan peeḍayetkṛpaṇam janam
Kṛpaṇaḥ peeḍyamaanaḥ svamṛtyunaa hanti paarthivam.

The ruler who did not expand his armed forces,
Who did not conquer other rulers and make them pay taxes,
Who did not protect his people well,
Is as useless as an oilless sesame seed.

In a country ruled by unrighteous rulers,
there is no timely rain, the land is not productive,
the nation declines, enemies increase and wealth diminishes.

A ruler should never give up courage, learning, eloquence, generosity, strength, valour, and ambition (to conquer).

A ruler should not bear lust for union with others' women, greed for others' wealth or anger in meting out punishment to people.

The ruler should not, out of self-interest, trouble poor people, for the troubled poor, when they die, kill the ruler as well.

सदुपायैश्च सन्मन्त्रैः कार्यसिद्धिरथोद्यमैः
भवेदल्पजनस्यापि किं पुनर्नृपतेर्न हि।।

Sadupaayaiścha sanmantraiḥ kaaryasiddhirathodyamaiḥ
Bhavedalpajanasyaapi kim punarnṛpaterna hi.

सुराप्यपि वरो राजा न स्त्रैणो नातिकोपवान्
लोकांश्चण्डस्तापयति स्त्रैणो वर्णान् विलुम्पति।।

Suraapyapi varo raajaa na straiṇo naatikopavaan
Lokaamśchaṇḍastaapayati straiṇo varṇaan vilumpati.

राज्यवृक्षस्य नृपतिर्मूलं स्कन्धाश्च मन्त्रिणः
शाखाः सेनाधिपाः सेनाः पल्लवाः कुसुमानि च
प्रजाः फलानि भूभागा बीजं भूमिः प्रकल्पिता।।

Raajyavṛkshasya nṛpatirmoolam skandhaaścha mantriṇaḥ
Śaakhaaḥ senaadhipaaḥ senaaḥ pallavaaḥ kusumaani cha
Prajaaḥ phalaani bhoobhaagaa beejam bhoomiḥ prakalpitaa.

स्वेष्टहानिकरः शत्रुर्दुष्टः पापप्रचारवान्
इष्टसम्पादनं न्याय्यं प्रजानां पालनं हि तत्।।

Sveshṭahaanikaraḥ śatrurdushṭaḥ paapaprachaaravaan
Ishṭasampaadanam nyaayyam prajaanaam paalanam hi tat.

Through good devices, good counsel and good effort,
even the common people achieve things.
What about rulers then? (Undoubtedly they will achieve success.)

It is preferable that a ruler drinks and is not a womaniser or an excessively angry person,
since an excessively angry ruler troubles the people, and the womanising ruler disrupts the social fabric.

If the state is a tree, the root of that tree is the ruler,
the trunk is counsellors, branches are army chiefs, the leaves are armies, the flowers are the people, the fruits are the revenue from the land and the seed is the territory.

He who stands against the fulfilment of one's desires is an enemy. One who spreads sin is an evil one.
Fulfilment of the legitimate aspirations of the people is protection of the people by the ruler.

## SEARCH

योग्येकान्तं च कुलटा जारं वैद्यं च व्याधितः
धृतपण्यो महार्घत्वं दानशीलस्तु याचकम्
रक्षितारं मृगयते भीतिश्छिद्रं तु दुर्जनः।।

Yogyekaantam cha kulaṭaa jaaram vaidyam cha vyādhitaḥ
Dhṛtapaṇyo mahaarghatvam daanaśeelastu yaachakam
Rakshitaaram mṛgayate bheetiśchidram tu durjanaḥ.

## SECRECY

आयुर्वित्तं गृहच्छिद्रं मन्त्रमैथुन भेषजम्
दानमानापमानं च नवैतानि सुगोपयेत्।।

Aayurvittam gṛhacchidram mantramaithuna bheshajam
Daanamaanaapamaanam cha navaitaani sugopayet.

## SELF

आत्मैव ह्यात्मनः साक्षी गतिरात्मैव ह्यात्मनः
मावमंस्थास्त्वमात्मानं नृणां साक्षित्वमुत्तमम्।।

Aatmaiva hyaatmanaḥ sākshee gatiraatmaiva hyaatmanaḥ
Maavamamsthaastvamātmaanam nṛṇaam saakshitv-amuttamam.

## SERVANT

भृतिदानेन सन्तुष्टा मानेन परिवर्धिताः
सान्त्विता मृदुवाचा ये न त्यजन्त्यधिपं हि ते।।

Bhṛtidaanena santushṭaa maanena parivardhitaaḥ
Saantvitaa mṛduvaachaa ye na tyajantyadhipam hi te.

## SEARCH

The yogi seeks solitude,
the hooker a customer,
the patient a physician,
the shopkeeper inflation,
the generous donor the beggar,
the one who is afraid, a protector,
and wicked ones quarrels.

## SECRECY

Nine things should be kept secret:
Age, wealth, dissensions in the family, mantra, sexual union, medicine, donation, respect and disrespect.

## SELF

The Self (Soul) alone is one's witness, the Self is one's guide and goal,
Hence never disregard the Self, the supreme witness of human beings.

## SERVANT

If satisfied with timely wages, encouraged by respect and pacified by sweet words, a servant never leaves his master.

## SILENCE

यत्कर्तव्यं न जानाति कृतं जानाति चेतरः
नैव वक्ति च कर्तव्यं कृतं यश्चोत्तमो नरः।।

Yatkartavyam na jaanaati kṛtam jaanaati chetaraḥ
Naiva vakti cha kartavyam kṛtam yaśchottamo naraḥ.

## SINS

हिंसास्तेयान्यथाकामपैशुन्यं परुषानृतम्
सम्भिन्नालापव्यापादममिथ्यादृग्विपर्ययम्
पापकर्मेति दशधा कायवाङ्मानसैस्त्यजेत्।।

Himsaasteyaanyathaakaamapaiśunyam parushaanṛtam
Sambhinnaalaapavyaapaadamamithyaadṛgviparyayam
Paapakarmeti daśadhaa kaayavaangmaanasaistyajet.

## SON

संप्राप्य महतीं वृद्धिं वर्तेत पितुराज्ञया
पुत्रस्य पितुराज्ञाहि परमं भूषणं स्मृतम्।।

Sampraapya mahateem vṛddhim varteta pituraajñayaa
Putrasya pituraajñaahi paramam bhooshaṇam smṛtam.

## START UP

नारम्भो बहुकार्याणामेकदैव सुखावहः
नारम्भितसमाप्तिं तु विना चान्यं समाचरेत्।।

Naarambho bahukaaryaaṇaamekadaiva sukhaavahaḥ
Naarambhitasamaaptim tu vinaa chaanyam amaacharet.

## SILENCE

He is the superior person who does not talk about what he intends to do or what he has done,
for then what he intends to do will not be known and only a few will know what he has done.

## SINS

Violence, theft, adultery, depravity, harsh speech, falsehood, wounding people with insincere words, arrogance, atheism, acting contrarily,
these ten are sins.
One should reject these ten sins in mind, word and deed.

## SON

Even after attaining great prosperity, a son should act according to his father's command, since for a son obeying a father's command is deemed the supreme ornament.

## START UP

Starting too many things simultaneously does not conduce to happiness. Without finishing a job already started, a new job should not be started.

## TRANSIENCE

यौवनं जीवितं चित्तं छाया लक्ष्मीश्च स्वामिता
चञ्चलानि षडेतानि ज्ञात्वा धर्मरतो भवेत्।।

Yauvanam jeevitam chittam cchaayaa lakshmeeścha swaamitaa
Chañchalaani shaḍetaani jñaatvaa dharmarato bhavet.

## VIGILANCE

स्वकार्ये शिथिलो यः स्यात् किमन्ये न भवन्ति हि
जागरूकः स्वकार्ये यस्तत्सहायाश्च तत्समाः।।

Svakaarye śithilo yaḥ syaat kimanye na bhavanti hi
Jaagarookaḥ svakaarye yastatsahaayaaścha tatsamaaḥ.

## WEALTH

सुभार्यापुत्रमित्रार्थं हितं नित्यं धनार्जनम्
दानार्थं च बिना त्वेतैः किं धनैश्च जनैश्च किम्।।

Subhaaryāputramitrārtham hitam nityam dhanaarjanam
Daanaartham cha binaa tvetaiḥ kim dhanaiścha janaiścha kim.

## WISE ONES

अवमानं पुरस्कृत्य मानं कृत्वा तु पृष्ठतः
स्वकार्यं साधयेत् प्राज्ञः कार्यध्वंसो हि मूर्खता।।

Avamaanam puraskṛtya mānam kṛtvaa tu pṛshṭhataḥ
Svakaaryam saadhayet praajñaḥ kaaryadhwamso hi moo-
rkhataa.

ह्यधिकोऽस्मीति सर्वेभ्यो ह्यधिकज्ञानवानहम्
धर्मतत्त्वमिदमिति नैवं मन्येत बुद्धिमान्।।

Hyadhikoasmeeti sarvebhyo hyadhikajñaanavaanaham
Dharmatattvamidamiti naivam manyeta buddhimaan.

## TRANSIENCE

Youth, life, mind, shadow, riches and ruling power, these six are transient and unsteady.
Knowing this, one should remain addicted to righteousness.

## VIGILANCE

If one is indifferent about one's own affairs, how else will others be?
If one is vigilant about one's own affairs, the servants will also be likewise.

## WEALTH

One should daily earn wealth, for the sake of a good spouse, good children and good friends,
If these do not exist, what is the use of wealth or servants?

## WISE ONES

The wise one will achieve his task, disregarding disrespect, and giving pride the backseat,
Ruining one's task (out of pride or self-regard) is foolishness.

The wise one should never think: "I am greater than everyone", "I have more knowledge than others" and "This is the essence of righteousness".

विद्या शौर्यं च दाक्ष्यं च बलं धैर्यं च पञ्चमम्
मित्राणि सहजान्याहुर्वर्तयन्ति हि तैर्बुधाः।।

Vidyaa śauryam cha daakshyam cha balam dhairyam cha pañchamam
Mitraaṇi sahajaanyaahurvartayanti hi tairbudhaaḥ.

नोपेक्षेत स्त्रियं बालं रोगं दासं पशुं धनम्
विद्याभ्यासं क्षणमपि सत्सेवां बुद्धिमान्नरः।।

Nopeksheta striyam baalam rogam daasam paśum dhanam
Vidyaabhyaasam kshaṇamapi satsevaam buddhimaannaraḥ.

भूत्वा महाधनः सम्यक् पोष्यवर्गं तु पोषयेत्
अदत्वा यत्किञ्चिदपि न नयेद्दिवसं बुधः।।

Bhootvaa mahaadhanaḥ samyak poshyavargam tu poshayet
Adatvaa yatkiñchidapi na nayeddivasam budhaḥ.

अपि स्थाणुवदासीत शुष्यन्परिगतः क्षुधा
त त्वेवानर्थसम्पन्नां वृत्तिमीहेत पण्डितः।।

Api sthaaṇuvadaaseeta śushyanparigataḥ kshudhaa
Ta tvevānarthasampannaam vṛttimeeheta paṇḍitaḥ.

## WISE WORDS

मदरकतस्य हंसस्य कोकिलस्य शिखण्डिनः
हरन्ति न तथा वाचो यथा वाचो विपश्चिताम्।।

Madarakatasya hamsasya kokilasya śikhaṇḍinaḥ
Haranti na tathaa vaacho yathaa vācho vipaśchitaam.

Learning, daring, skill, strength and courage—these five are one's natural friends, for with the help of these, wise ones lead their lives well.

The wise one should not, even for a moment, neglect his woman, son, disease, servant, cattle, wealth, learning or serving good ones.

When one becomes very wealthy, one should look after one's dependants. Without gifting away something, the wise one should not spend a single day.

The wise one will not desire an unrighteous means of livelihood, even if he is reduced by hunger to the state of a dried stick.

**WISE WORDS**

The cooings of the lovestruck swan, Koel or the peacock do not captivate men to the same extent as the words of learned scholars.

## WITNESS

सत्येन पूयते साक्षी धर्मः सत्येन वर्धते
तस्मात् सत्यं हि वक्तव्यं सर्ववर्णेषु साक्षिभिः।।

Satyena pooyate saakshee dharmaḥ satyena vardhate
Tasmaat satyam hi vaktavyam sarvavarṇeshu saakshibhiḥ.

मन्यते वै पापकारी न कश्चित् पश्यतीति माम्
तांश्च देवाः प्रपश्यन्ति तथा ह्यन्तरपूरुषः।।

Manyate vai paapakaaree na kaśchit paśyateeti maam
Taamścha devaaḥ prapaśyanti tathaa hyantarapoorushaḥ.

## WRONG ACTION

असत्कार्यनियोकतारं गुरुं वापि प्रबोधयेत्
नातिक्रामेदपि लघुं क्वचित् सत्कार्यबोधकम्।।

Asatkaaryaniyokataaram gurum vaapi prabodhayet
Naatikraamedapi laghum kvachit satkāryabodhakam.

## WITNESS

A witness is respected for truth.
Righteousness increases by truth.
Hence truth should be told by witnesses, to whatever social ladder they belong.

The one who sins thinks that no one is watching,
but the angels and the immanent Supreme Person (God) watches everything.

## WRONG ACTION

Even a teacher who incites you to wrong action should be made to understand (that his direction will not be carried out),
Even a young boy who gives advice to do the right thing should be obeyed.

## INDEX (SUBJECTWISE)